T0167765

Bankruptcy *Not* Bailout

WORKING GROUP ON ECONOMIC POLICY

Many of the writings associated with this Working Group will be published by the Hoover Institution Press or other publishers. Materials published to date, or in production, are listed below. Books that are part of the Working Group on Economic Policy's *Resolution Project* are marked with an asterisk.

*Bankruptcy Not Bailout: A Special Chapter 14**
Edited by Kenneth E. Scott and John B. Taylor

Government Policies and the Delayed Economic Recovery
Edited by Lee E. Ohanian, John B. Taylor, and Ian J. Wright

Why Capitalism?
Allan H. Meltzer

First Principles: Five Keys to Restoring America's Prosperity
John B. Taylor

*Ending Government Bailouts as We Know Them**
Edited by Kenneth E. Scott, George P. Shultz, and John B. Taylor

*How Big Banks Fail: And What to Do about It**
Darrell Duffie

The Squam Lake Report: Fixing the Financial System
Darrell Duffie, *et al.*

Getting Off Track: How Government Actions and Interventions Caused, Prolonged, and Worsened the Financial Crisis
John B. Taylor

The Road Ahead for the Fed
Edited by John B. Taylor and John D. Ciorciari

Putting Our House in Order: A Guide to Social Security and Health Care Reform
George P. Shultz and John B. Shoven

Bankruptcy
Not Bailout

A Special Chapter 14

Edited by

Kenneth E. Scott

John B. Taylor

Contributing Authors

Andrew Crockett

Darrell Duffie

Thomas H. Jackson

William F. Kroener III

Kenneth E. Scott

David Skeel

Kimberly Anne Summe

John B. Taylor

Kevin M. Warsh

HOOVER INSTITUTION PRESS

Stanford University | Stanford, California

www.hoover.org

Hoover Institution Press Publication No. 625

Hoover Institution at Leland Stanford Junior University,
Stanford, California 94305-6010

First printing 2012
19   18   17   16   15   14   13   12   9   8   7   6   5   4   3   2

Manufactured in the United States of America

The paper used in this publication meets the minimum Requirements of the American National Standard for Information Sciences—Permanence of Paper for Printed Library Materials, ANSI/NISO Z39.48-1992. ∞

Cataloging-in-Publication Data is available from the Library of Congress.

ISBN 978-0-8179-1514-8 (cloth.: alk. paper)
ISBN 978-0-8179-1516-2 (e-book versions)

*The Hoover Institution gratefully acknowledges
the following individuals and foundations
for their significant support of the*
WORKING GROUP ON ECONOMIC POLICY

Lynde and Harry Bradley Foundation
John A. Gunn and Cynthia Fry Gunn
Stephen and Sarah Page Herrick

Contents

Preface

John B. Taylor

> Let's write Chapter 14 into the law so that we have a credible
> alternative to bailouts in practice. We can then be ready to use
> a rules-based bankruptcy process to allow financial firms to fail
> without causing financial disruption.
> —*George P. Shultz*

The purpose of this book is to introduce and analyze a new and
more predictable bankruptcy process designed specifically for large
financial institutions. We call the new bankruptcy law "Chapter
14" because it is currently an unused chapter number of the U.S.
Bankruptcy Code. The new proposal will create greater financial
stability and reduce the likelihood of bailouts.

Chapter 14 represents the outcome of extensive collaborative research by lawyers, economists, financial market experts, and policy
makers—many of whom are contributors to this book. Much of the
work has taken place during the three years since *Ending Government Bailouts as We Know Them* (edited by Kenneth Scott, George
Shultz, and John Taylor) was written in 2009. Indeed, this new
book is a follow-up to that earlier endeavor, incorporating more
detailed research findings, and also considering the implications of
the so-called "orderly liquidation authority" in Title II of the Dodd-
Frank Wall Street Reform and Consumer Protection Act, which
was passed in 2010.

The book starts off with Kenneth Scott's summary of the key
legal and economic differences between the new orderly liquidation

authority and the proposed new Chapter 14 bankruptcy process. The orderly liquidation authority increases uncertainty, raises due process issues, creates additional incentives to bail out large financial institutions, and increases moral hazard. Title II of the Dodd-Frank bill gives the government considerable power and discretion to intervene, take over, and liquidate financial companies with no role for meaningful judicial review or analysis. Even with the best of intentions, it is difficult to see how the Federal Deposit Insurance Corporation (FDIC), the agency assigned by the law to this job, can run such a liquidation process for large, complex financial institutions in a predictable rulelike manner, which is so important for the smooth operation of financial markets.

Chapter 14 would give the government a viable alternative to Title II and thereby avoid these problems. Even if the discretionary bailout option remained in the law through the new orderly liquidation authority, government officials might well find Chapter 14 more attractive—because of its more predictable rules-based features—and thereby choose this option rather than a bailout. At the least, there would be a credible alternative to a bailout, which would make bailouts less likely. As described in the quote at the start of this preface by former Secretary of Treasury, State, and Labor George P. Shultz, Chapter 14 would give the government the option of letting a failing financial firm go into bankruptcy in a predictable, rules-based way without having to cause spillovers to the economy. If possible, it would also permit people to continue to use the company's financial services—just as people continue to fly when an airline company is in bankruptcy reorganization. Creating this option thus puts incentives in place that tend to drive government officials away from the oft-chosen bailout route.

The centerpiece of the book is Tom Jackson's detailed description of Chapter 14, which would differ from current bankruptcy law under Chapter 7 and Chapter 11 in several ways. It would create a group of judges to specialize in financial markets and institutions, which would be responsible for handling the bankruptcy of a large financial firm. A common perception is that bankruptcy is too slow to deal with systemic risk situations in large complex institutions, but under the proposal, there would be the ability to proceed immediately.

In addition to the typical bankruptcy commencement by creditors, an involuntary proceeding could be initiated by a government regulatory agency. Moreover, the government or creditors could propose a reorganization plan—not simply a liquidation. An important advantage of this bankruptcy approach is that debtors and creditors negotiate with clear rules and judicial review throughout the process. In contrast, the orderly liquidation authority is less transparent, with more discretion by government officials and few opportunities for review. Chapter 14 relies more on the rule of law and less on discretion.

Following the central description of Chapter 14, the book then reviews various issues that arise in practice. William Kroener delves into the problems of how orderly liquidation would work in practice under the authority of the FDIC, showing some of the advantages of Chapter 14. Kimberly Summe examines how the Lehman Brothers' derivatives portfolio would have worked out under the existing Bankruptcy Code if Dodd-Frank had been in effect in September 2008. She concludes that for any failed "systemically important" financial company captured by Dodd-Frank, the orderly resolution authority would not have resulted in any substantial change in the way derivative trades are handled postbankruptcy. In other words, the workout process for derivatives would not have proceeded much differently under Dodd-Frank. However, the orderly liquidation authority combined with the new requirement to place derivative contracts at clearinghouses would likely lead to a significant probability that such a clearinghouse would be bailed out by the government.

In a revealing dialogue on the costs and benefits of automatic stays in the case of repurchase agreements and derivatives, Darrell Duffie and David Skeel show that the proposed Chapter 14 resolves many complex incentive issues simply by adhering to the basic legal principles of the Bankruptcy Code with small adjustments to prevent runs and/or reduce incentives for excess risk taking. The chapter by Kenneth Scott and Tom Jackson then argues that Chapter 14 can preserve the going-concern value of a failed financial institution as well as or better than the FDIC would under Title II of Dodd-Frank. In the short chapter that follows, Ken Scott elaborates on the reasons why the new liquidation authority would likely violate constitutional due process requirements in practice. But one of the most important questions is how Chapter 14 would work in the midst of a financial crisis, a topic that is addressed in the final two chapters by two former top financial officials: Kevin Warsh and Andrew Crockett.

Although the chapters in this book are authored by individual researchers, they represent the collaborative work of the Resolution Project at Stanford University's Hoover Institution. The Project has included Andrew Crockett, Darrell Duffie, Richard J. Herring, Thomas Jackson, William F. Kroener, Kenneth E. Scott, George P. Shultz, David Skeel, Kimberly Anne Summe, and John B. Taylor, with Kenneth Scott serving as chair.

Part A

A NEW BANKRUPTCY APPROACH

1

A Guide to the Resolution of Failed Financial Institutions

Dodd-Frank Title II and Proposed Chapter 14

KENNETH E. SCOTT

I. BACKGROUND

The "Resolution Project" began in August 2009, in the midst of the financial crisis, to consider how best to deal with the failure of major financial institutions. The members of the group, assembled from institutions across the country, were Andrew Crockett, Darrell Duffie, Richard Herring, Thomas Jackson, William Kroener, Kenneth Scott (chair), George Shultz, Kimberly Summe, and John Taylor, later joined by David Skeel.[1] A number of meetings and discussions led to papers and then a conference in December 2009, followed by a book: *Ending Government Bailouts as We Know Them.*[2]

The heated debate in Congress over the proper response continued until July 2010, culminating in the Dodd-Frank Wall Street Reform and Consumer Protection Act (Pub. L. 111–203). This massive statute runs for 848 pages, contains 16 titles, requires 386 more agency rulemakings, and mandates 67 studies. Most of it was a

---

1. Biographical information may be found at the end of this volume.
2. Kenneth Scott, George Shultz, & John Taylor, eds., *Ending Government Bailouts as We Know Them* (Hoover Institution Press, 2010).

collection of assorted changes to the financial system that various groups had been advocating for some time, unrelated to the causes of the panic.

A popular conception, in the press and Congress, of the cause of the panic was that when the investment bank Lehman Brothers failed in September 2008, it had to be put into bankruptcy reorganization because (unlike commercial banks) it could not be taken over by the Federal Deposit Insurance Corporation (FDIC). Whatever its merits, that view provided much of the impetus for the enactment of Titles I (Financial Stability) and II (Orderly Liquidation Authority) of the Dodd-Frank Act, which were intended to prevent the failure of systemically important (nonbank) financial institutions (SIFIs) and, if that was unsuccessful, provide for a new failure procedure whereby the Secretary of the Treasury could institute the takeover of a SIFI with the FDIC becoming the receiver.

Title I created a new Financial Stability Oversight Council composed of the heads of various financial regulatory agencies, which is to collect data about financial companies and financial risks and to identify financial companies that could pose a threat to U.S. financial stability. Such companies would be supervised by the Federal Reserve Board (the "Fed") and subjected to a list of more stringent prudential standards and requirements.

Title II authorizes the Secretary of the Treasury, upon recommendation by the Fed and FDIC, to determine that a financial company is in default or in danger of a default that would have serious adverse effects on U.S. financial stability, and then to petition the DC district court to appoint the FDIC as receiver to "liquidate" the company. Title II, and not the Bankruptcy Code, would govern the receivership.

The Resolution Project group turned its focus to the development of a supplemental proposal for a modified bankruptcy law, denominated as a new Chapter 14,[3] designed exclusively for major financial institutions. This paper is written for a moderately knowledgeable audience and is intended to identify and compare the major differences in the Dodd-Frank Title II and Chapter 14 procedures and to outline the reasons why the group believes the latter to be preferable. Sections 202 and 216 of the Dodd-Frank Act (the "Act") called for an inquiry on bankruptcy resolution to be conducted by the Government Accountability Office (GAO), the Federal Reserve System (FRS) Board of Governors, and the Administrative Office of the United States Courts, and one of the Resolution Project's goals was to make a contribution to that analysis and its consideration by the Congress.[4]

II. OBJECTIVES OF RESOLUTION LAW FOR MAJOR INSOLVENT FINANCIAL FIRMS

Any failure law for business firms has a number of objectives, not always fully consistent. One is to provide a mechanism for collective action by creditors to realize on the assets of the firm in an orderly manner, as opposed to an individual scramble for whatever could be seized and sold first, and apply the proceeds to claims in accordance with the contractual priorities for which they had bargained and charged. An efficient procedure for maximizing recoveries, involving

---

3. The current version (previously entitled Chapter 11F), primarily authored by Thomas H. Jackson following extensive discussion and input from the other members of the Resolution Project, is included as chapter 2 in this volume.

4. The agency reports when submitted did not make recommendations but surveyed the principal issues and arguments. The project's proposals are reviewed at some length in the Federal Reserve Board's (FRB's) "Study on the Resolution of Financial Companies under the Bankruptcy Code" (July 2011).

notices and hearings, contributes to meeting expectations and reducing losses, and hence to lower costs of capital for the carrying on
of all business enterprises.

A second objective, which could be seen as an adjunct to the
first, is to retain the "going-concern value" of any parts of the business that can still be operated at a net profit through a "reorganization" of the firm, as opposed to the liquidation sale of its various
assets. This is particularly significant for financial firms, much of
whose value lies in the organization, knowledge, and services of
its personnel and their relationships to clients, rather than in
separately salable assets like inventory, real estate, buildings, and
machinery.

A third objective, perhaps uniquely so for "systemically important financial institutions," is to avoid a breakdown of the entire
financial system. What this means and what it entails is considered
toward the end of this chapter. So we turn next to an examination
of the differences between the Act and Chapter 14, necessarily limiting it to central concepts and omitting a host of (not at all unimportant) details.[5]

III. FINANCIAL INSTITUTIONS COVERED

A. Dodd-Frank

The Act excludes from its coverage banks and (notably)
government-sponsored entities (such as Fannie Mae and Freddie

---

5. Broker-dealers and insurance companies have special, separate provisions in
the Act.

Mac),[6] and includes in its coverage companies predominately (on the basis of either assets or revenues) engaged in financial activities. From the large universe of financial companies, the Fed is supposed to give especially intensive supervision to all bank holding companies with more than $50 billion in consolidated assets and those financial companies that the Financial Stability Oversight Council has selected as potentially posing a threat to U.S. financial stability in the event of its financial distress.[7] But whether or not so predesignated or supervised, *any* financial company that the Secretary of the Treasury determines to be in danger of default with serious adverse effects on financial stability[8] may be seized and put into FDIC receivership by petition to the DC district court.[9] Financial companies that are not so chosen would remain under the existing Bankruptcy Code. In other words, application of Title II of the Act is left to administrative discretion, defined only by "findings" that the agency itself makes at the time of action, and counterparties have no way of knowing in advance which law will apply.

B. Chapter 14

The new Chapter applies to all financial companies and their subsidiaries with more than $100 billion in consolidated assets. Counterparties would generally not be left in doubt as to which companies will be subject to a special resolution procedure and

---

6. The latter is a major omission, since the Congressional Budget Office (CBO) estimated in August 2009 that their losses would cost taxpayers more than $290 billion, far more than the cost of assistance to all other financial companies combined.

7. § 113(a)(1). All section references are to the Dodd-Frank Act, Pub. L. 111–203 (July 21, 2010).

8. § 203(b).

9. § 202(a).

which ones will be dealt with under the Bankruptcy Code provisions. Uncertainty in financial transactions increases risk and costs for everyone, and is to be minimized wherever possible.

IV. COMMENCEMENT OF PROCEEDINGS

A. Dodd-Frank

The Act creates an elaborate and potentially cumbersome bureaucratic process for triggering seizure of a financial company. The Fed and FDIC (or other primary federal regulator) jointly make a recommendation to the Treasury Secretary, based upon consideration of a list of factors that includes the reason why proceeding under the Bankruptcy Code is not appropriate. The Treasury Secretary then must make seven findings, including that the firm is a financial company projected to be in danger of a default (because of insufficient capital or ability to pay its obligations when due) that, if handled under the Bankruptcy Code, would have serious adverse effects on U.S. financial stability.[10]

The Secretary thereupon files a petition in the DC district court to appoint the FDIC as its receiver (unless the company's board consents). The statute mandates that within 24 hours: (1) there is a closed and secret hearing in which the Secretary presents all the accumulated documentation underlying the agency recommendations and his conclusions, (2) the company can try to present a rebuttal as to its portfolio asset valuations and capital or access to liquidity, (3) the judge considers all the conflicting evidence (but

---

10. § 203(b).

only on two of the seven mandatory determinations), and (4) the court issues either an order authorizing the receivership or a written opinion giving all reasons supporting a denial of the petition. If the district court cannot accomplish all that within 24 hours, the petition is granted by operation of law.[11] Apart from the obvious impossibility of an effective rebuttal by the company—much less of findings of fact and a reasoned decision by the court—within such a truncated time frame, any appeal to a higher court would be limited to that one-sided, one-day record, and any stay of the liquidation is prohibited.[12] This summary procedure raises substantial constitutional problems under the Due Process Clause, which could invalidate the entire Title II mechanism.[13]

B. Chapter 14

To the involuntary procedure in current bankruptcy law, initiated by unpaid creditors, there is added authority for the financial institution's primary regulator to commence a case both on the grounds applicable to other involuntary petitions as well as on the ground of "balance sheet" insolvency: its assets are less than its liabilities or it has unreasonably small capital. This is analogous to the "in default or in danger of default" concept in Dodd-Frank,[14] but the company has an actual opportunity in a court to challenge the assertion (in closed and secret hearing, should the judge deem appropriate), without a truncated time frame, if it really disputes the adverse judgments on its financial soundness or believes the

---

11. § 202(a)(1)(A)(v).

12. § 202(a)(1)(B).

13. For discussion, *see* Kenneth E. Scott, *Dodd-Frank: Resolution or Expropriation?* chapter 7 in this volume.

14. § 203(c)(4).

administrative valuations of its illiquid (nontraded) assets are demonstrably erroneous.

Chapter 14 retains the ability of the management of a firm to itself initiate a voluntary proceeding in lieu of having to go into FDIC receivership. If the management sees the firm's financial position as becoming untenable, it does not have to wait for balance sheet insolvency or default on obligations, but can inaugurate a reorganization to try to salvage in part its business and retain its jobs. Much recent history indicates the tendency of banking regulators for various reasons not to take over prior to complete insolvency (as the FDIC Improvement Act of 1991 authorized them to do) but to wait until losses to the deposit insurance fund have become substantial despite its supervisory powers and stake as the primary creditor. The Dodd-Frank seizure procedure was designed to require a consensus of a set of government agencies before taking action. The history of voluntary bankruptcy, conversely, is replete with examples of preemptive action in which asset values are written down, there is a negotiation to allocate losses among claimants (with stockholders being the first to go), and a reduced business continues in successful operation, sometimes under existing management (which, as explained subsequently, Dodd-Frank makes very unlikely). Incentives for management to act in a fashion more timely than receivership liquidation are socially valuable.

V. THE RESOLUTION PROCEDURE

A. Dodd-Frank: FDIC as Receiver

One of the reasons stressed in Congress for enactment of Title II was the FDIC's long experience in liquidating failed commercial banks. But the SIFIs with which the Act is primarily concerned are giant firms—hundreds of billions or even trillions of dollars in size, with any commercial bank as only one part of the complex. The FDIC's experience has been in dealing with numerous small and medium-sized banks, in which it is by far the biggest creditor through the deposit insurance fund, and for which there are often obvious— and larger—institutions ready to take over; only in the last several years has it encountered a few very large ones, with a wider variety of assets and claimants.[15] And in the case of a common reassess- ment type of systemic event (see section VI.A of this chapter), the FDIC might have to take on a number of such institutions at the same time—a situation for which no one has experience or existing capacity.

The Act mandates that the seized financial company shall be liquidated;[16] it may not be reorganized, and the management "re- sponsible" must be immediately removed.[17] It is evident that the mandate was intended to be more punitive than value enhancing. There may be indirect ways to avoid its needless value destruc- tion, but it is certainly not conducive to efficient resolution, a pro- cess that the Act recognizes could take more than five years to complete.[18]

More troubling is the power of the receiver to operate without transparency and not observe standard bankruptcy rules intended to adhere to absolute priority of claims and equal treatment of claim- ants in the same category. (Although many of the relevant Title II provisions have been imported from the Bankruptcy Code, provisions

---

15. For a fuller discussion, *see* David Skeel, *The New Financial Deal* 117–27 (John Wiley & Sons, 2010).

16. § 214.

17. § 206.

18. § 202(d).

for judicial hearings, management participation, and creditor votes were not.) The Act authorizes the FDIC, as it sees fit, to transfer assets *and liabilities* to a "bridge" institution where they are fully protected,[19] and depart from equal treatment of unsecured receivership claimants if it decides that would be good for the receivership estate.[20] If those dealing with a large financial institution have to calculate the risk they are assuming not only on the basis of business assessments but also on predictions of the exercise of legally unreviewable political discretion rather than on reasonably settled legal rules, a major cost and burden is imposed on the operation of financial markets.

B. Chapter 14

Bankruptcy judges have been handling the liquidation and reorganization of very large and complicated companies for decades. Nonetheless, it should be recognized that giant financial firms pose some particular issues. Therefore, Chapter 14 contemplates the development of a small (hopefully, cases will be few and infrequent) and specialized panel of district and bankruptcy court judges and special masters that would oversee these cases. Like the FDIC, this panel would have to develop some special expertise with giant SIFIs over time. The details are spelled out in chapter 2.

In a typical Bankruptcy Code proceeding, management (as the "debtor-in-possession" or "DIP") remains in control of ordinary business operations, and has an exclusive period in which to file a plan of reorganization. Upon creditor petition, the bankruptcy court may

---

19. § 210(h)(1).

20. § 210(b)(4). The FDIC has adopted a rule stating that it will not use its authority to depart from equal treatment for holders of long-term senior debt or subordinated debt, or shareholders. 12 C.F.R. § 380.27.

turn control over to a bankruptcy "trustee." Under Chapter 14, the financial company's primary federal regulator could initiate the proceeding, and could petition to have the FDIC appointed as a trustee. The FDIC would then function under Chapter 14 and therefore have the option (lacking in Title II of the Act) to pursue openly a traditional reorganization to maximize the business's value for benefit of creditors, rather than being forced to liquidate it in a formal sense to satisfy § 214. In addition, there would be no period of exclusivity in Chapter 14 in which only management could propose a plan of reorganization; both the FDIC and a creditor's committee would be given concurrent rights to file such a plan.

Whoever is in charge, resolution under Chapter 14 would be conducted under established (Chapters 11 and 7) bankruptcy rules about absolute priority, avoiding powers, transfers, and preferences (except as noted in section VI.C herein). Dispositions of cash and of assets outside the ordinary course of business require creditor notice and opportunity for hearing, particularly on the value being received. Plans of reorganization, with their allocation of losses among claimant classes, are subject to approval votes and judicial oversight. The resolution would proceed in the open, unlike present FDIC practices.

These requirements constitute safeguards against not only erroneous administrative judgments but also political manipulation and favoritism of selected interests. That such concerns are not merely speculative is illustrated by the way the government managed the Chrysler bankruptcy under the current Bankruptcy Code to avoid creditor voting rights.[21] This defect is partially addressed in the new Chapter 14 through the provisions entrusting this category of

---

21. Mark J. Roe & David Skeel, *Assessing the Chrysler Bankruptcy*, 108 Mich. L. Rev. 727 (2010).

cases to Article III judges with life tenure. In addition, other broader safeguards are included to ensure that sales under Section 363 of the Bankruptcy Code do not, sub rosa, avoid the safeguards of voting under plans of reorganization and protection of dissenting creditors.

VI. SYSTEMIC RISK—BREAKDOWN OF THE FINANCIAL SYSTEM

A. Concepts of Systemic Risk—What Exactly Is the Scenario?

Systemic risk is much referred to but typically not defined operationally or modeled in any generally accepted form.[22] At least three different (if at times overlapping) notions can be found.[23] All describe paths to the failure, or failure to function, of a large number of major financial institutions and a breakdown of the system for allocating financial credit.

Type 1: Macro Shocks—Massive losses or disruptions simultaneously affecting many key institutions in the economy. Suppose the 9/11 al-Qaeda attack had not been aimed at creating the dramatic psychological shock of the collapse of the World Trade Center towers, but instead at destroying the records and transactional capacity of the Federal Reserve Bank of New York and the New York and

---

22. John Taylor, *Defining Systemic Risk Operationally*, in *Ending Government Bailouts as We Know Them* (Kenneth Scott, George Shultz, & John Taylor eds., Hoover Institution Press, 2010).

23. George Kaufman & Kenneth Scott, *What Is Systemic Risk?* VII Independent Rev. 371 (2003).

NASDAQ stock exchanges. Or suppose, for a more recent example, the Japanese earthquake, tsunami, and nuclear power plant failure had all been centered in Tokyo instead of 150 miles to its north.

Type 2: Chain Reactions—"Domino" effects from the unexpected failure of a single giant institution. Losses from the initial collapse could cause some counterparties to become insolvent in turn, and the process could keep going outward from there. Some have seen the Lehman failure in this light, although in fact no significant counterparty was rendered insolvent.

Type 3: Common Reassessments—Affecting institutions with similar asset portfolios, whether or not directly linked. Thus, the rescues or collapses in a ten-day period in September 2008 of important institutions with large holdings of, or exposure to, (especially subprime) mortgage-backed securities (MBSs)—from the giant mortgage firms Fannie and Freddie to Merrill Lynch to Lehman Brothers to AIG—led banks and financial institutions throughout the world to become uncertain of each other's solvency, and discontinue or sharply raise the price of extensions of credit. With credit flows greatly reduced, the crisis spread from the financial to the real economy, and a severe recession was under way.

The September 2008 panic thus seems to belong mostly in the third category. Inadequate disclosure of specifics of hundreds of billions of dollars in loan and securities holdings, and skepticism as to their valuations on balance sheets, contributed greatly to the problem. Growing anxieties in 2007 about valuations led over time to MBSs becoming nearly untradable, which the Fed apparently perceived initially as due mainly to insufficient liquidity in the financial system, though it had tried to address that issue with a host of new lending facilities beginning in late 2007 and extending through

2008 into 2009.[24] But the September crunch had jolted financial institutions around the world into critically reassessing their counterparties' potential economic insolvency, and more liquidity did not remove that concern. In October 2008, the Treasury converted the Troubled Asset Relief Program (TARP) into capital investments of $10 to $25 billion in the six largest banks, which were more a signal of implied government guarantees against their failure than clearly sufficient by themselves to ensure their capital solvency against adverse portfolio outcomes. Far more important, the Fed purchased hundreds of billions of dollars of questionable securities.

B. Dodd-Frank

The concept of systemic risk underlying the Title II machinery is not explicit in either the Act or its legislative history, but it seems to correspond most closely to trying to prevent a Type 2 chain reaction, in accordance with the often-asserted myth that the cause of the panic was Lehman going into bankruptcy because the Treasury lacked the power to seize it. Lehman's failure was certainly one of the events that contributed to the September 2008 loss of confidence and panic, as discussed previously, but just why would subsequent receivership by the FDIC, instead of the bankruptcy court, have made a difference in that regard? No one would have been reassured about the composition and valuations of MBSs in others' portfolios, and the Act does nothing to cure the informational and valuation deficiencies that played a critical role in the credit crisis, beyond authorizing the Securities and Exchange Commission (SEC)

---

24. *See* the St. Louis Fed events timeline, available at http://timeline.stlouisfed .org.

to require some additional disclosure from issuers of asset-backed securities.[25] The resources that were deployed by the Fed to deal with what was a Type 3 common shock far exceed anything contemplated by Dodd-Frank and its Orderly Liquidation Fund.[26]

The Act requires SIFIs to prepare detailed resolution plans or "living wills" to facilitate their wind-downs, but on the basis that it occurs under the Bankruptcy Code and not a Title II receivership.[27] (And, if the problem is actually one of liquidity pressure on an otherwise solvent institution, the Act makes the problem worse by abolishing the Fed's § 13(3) emergency authority to act as a lender of last resort to a nonbank financial company.)[28]

Everyone proclaims that they are opposed to bailouts, but most seem to find it unnecessary to define what they are talking about. For my purposes, a bailout occurs when some favored claimants on a failed financial firm are given more than what they would receive in an ordinary bankruptcy, at the expense of others. The additional money might come from:

- the government: authorized expenditures by the Treasury (as in the Orderly Liquidation Fund), guarantee payments from the FDIC, or nonrecourse "loans" by the Fed;
- an "assessment" on prudent financial companies that did not fail;
- the receivership estate at the expense of disfavored creditors.

But whatever the source, moral hazard is created: the favored creditors have a reduced or no reason to pay attention to the behavior of

---

25. § 942.
26. § 210(n).
27. § 165(d)(4).
28. § 1101.

the debtor (now failed) firm, and the likelihood of such failures is increased.

Title II gives the FDIC power to obtain immediately from the Treasury financing funds equal to 10 percent of the (book) value of the seized firm,[29] and much more thereafter. Those funds may be made available to a "bridge" institution,[30] which can use them to pay liabilities transferred to it from the receivership. Therefore, perhaps the unstated premise is that under Title II, the FDIC would include all those significant financial counterparties that it thought might be endangered and immediately transfer their claims (and sufficient assets or advances to cover them in full), together with other liabilities, to a bridge bank, if it felt that was necessary to prevent a potential chain reaction of insolvencies. (That did not occur in the actual Lehman bankruptcy case, but put that aside.)

That would create two classes of general unsecured creditors of equal priority but different treatment: those transferred to the bridge company with full payment and those left behind in the receivership with partial recovery.[31] The Act requires that "similarly situated" creditors be treated in a "similar manner" *except* if the FDIC "determines" that preferences would increase net proceeds and the disfavored creditors would get at least what they would have received in a Chapter 7 liquidation.[32] (That determination and the selection of creditors to be favored are based upon unreviewable agency discretion.)[33]

---

29. § 210(n)(6).

30. § 210(h)(2)(G)(iv).

31. §§ 210(h)(5)(E), 210(d)(4).

32. §§ 210(b)(4), 210(d)(2).

33. A creditor can file suit to have a court determine the validity or amount of a claim against the failed institution (§ 210(a)(4)), but judicial review of the FDIC's decisions on claim transfers is prohibited. § 210(a)(9)(D)(ii).

That is possible, of course, only if liquidation under Title II would always yield enough—more than under the Bankruptcy Code—to cover the preferential payouts. Justifying that premise gives rise to an incentive—indeed, perhaps a necessity—for the FDIC in "determining" how much unsecured general creditors would have gotten in a hypothetical Chapter 7 liquidation to utilize unfavorable assumptions and produce a low figure, thereby increasing the scope of its ability to choose creditors to be paid the face value of their claims.

If the final result of asset liquidations and (if needed) certain creditor payment recoupments is insufficient for the receiver to fully repay its Treasury advances,[34] then a scheme is to be devised to assess the loss on the entire universe of SIFIs,[35] whether or not the causes of the initial failures lay in large part on government policies, as was true in 2008.[36]

The intention, stressed throughout the congressional consideration, is that taxpayers are not to bear the cost of a "bailout" of a financial company. But the real problem with bailouts comes from the protection of creditors, not stockholders (who are significantly or wholly wiped out in most bankruptcies). Shifting losses from taxpayers to an entire industry does not solve the problems arising from weakening or destroying the incentives of a firm's creditors to watch and restrain its risk taking.

A particular set of creditors deserves special attention in this regard: those who have entered into "qualified financial contracts" (QFCs) with a failed firm. QFCs include repos, interest rate and

---

34. The FDIC has five years or more to levy assessments on favored claimants to recover the excess they previously received over liquidation amounts. § 210(o)(1)(D)(i).

35. § 210(o)(4) contains a long list of "factors" to be taken into account in coming up with an actual plan.

36. *See* Kenneth Scott, *The Financial Crisis: Causes and Lessons*, 22 J. App. Corp. Fin. 22 (2010).

currency swaps, credit default swaps, and other derivatives; their notional amount has reached the hundreds of trillions of dollars. Title II of the Act carries forward most of their preferential treatment under current bankruptcy law. For these creditors, there is now an automatic one-day stay on collecting debts by terminating contracts and seizing and selling collateral, but they need not return prior (within 90 days) preferential payments or additional collateral, they have broader setoff rights, and so on. The complexity and legal status of Lehman's derivatives book—930,000 transactions— would be much the same under Title II as it was under the present Bankruptcy Code, where derivatives were terminated swiftly and efficiently but after three years claims are still being valued and settled.[37]

These provisions make the covered channels of short-term financing of a firm's operations much safer, and hence cheaper, but they also make its counterparties (who constitute the most sophisticated and best informed of all creditors) much more tolerant of its management's indulgence of risky strategies. There is an inherent trade-off at stake, and current QFC law leans heavily toward encouraging risk and discouraging market discipline.[38]

C. Chapter 14

As compared to the present Bankruptcy Code, limited creditor advances are facilitated if needed to reduce perceived contagion

---

37. Kimberly Ann Summe, *An Examination of Lehman Brothers' Derivatives Portfolio Postbankruptcy: Would Dodd-Frank Have Made a Difference?* chapter 4 in this volume.

38. Mark J. Roe, *The Derivatives Market's Payment Priorities as Financial Crisis Accelerator,* 63 Stan. L. Rev. 539–90 (2011); David Skeel & Thomas Jackson, *Transaction Consistency and the New Finance in Bankruptcy,* Penn. ILE Research Paper No. 11-06 (Feb. 2011), available at http:/ssrn.com/abstract=1773631, forthcoming in 112 Columbia L. Rev. 152 (2012).

concerns, but on the basis of a court hearing and approval (which can be quite speedy when justified) of the claimed need. Since reorganization is a permitted option rather than a formally prohibited one, DIP financing is expressly authorized to continue operations and can be given the priority of "administrative expenses."

There is a popular conception that there cannot be a successful reorganization of a failed SIFI, because counterparties would stop dealing with it. But postpetition creditors' unsecured claims, unlike their prepetition ones, go near the top of the payment priority ladder as "administrative expenses." If the government believes that systemic concerns are at stake, it could be authorized to provide subordinated DIP financing (along the lines of the Title II Orderly Liquidation Fund) in amounts more than adequate to cover all new claims and all assumed existing contracts.

Chapter 14 makes a distinction in the treatment of QFCs. Repos would be treated as secured loans, and the counterparty given the right to immediately sell the collateral *if* highly marketable securities (but not, for instance, MBSs, as the 2005 law authorized). This would preserve the use of repos as nearly risk-free short-term financing, but only under conditions where the sale of collateral would not have drastic market price effects. All other swaps and derivatives with a counterparty would be subject to a three-day stay, giving the debtor a window to assume (for example, if "in the money") or reject them all (or transfer them all in bulk to a new counterparty), and also subject to some preference limits. The objective is to make a somewhat different trade-off between efficient institutional financing and creditor monitoring incentives.[39]

---

39. For a fuller discussion, *see* Skeel & Jackson, *Transaction Consistency and the New Finance in Bankruptcy* (*supra* n. 38); and Darrell Duffie & David A. Skeel, *A Dialogue on the Costs and Benefits of Automatic Stays for Derivatives and Repurchase Agreements*, chapter 5 in this volume.

VII. CONCLUSIONS

A. Dodd-Frank

The Act places heavy reliance on agency discretion, not only in the hundreds of regulations yet to be issued dealing with the operation of financial firms and markets, but more specifically in the coverage of Title II resolution jurisdiction and the seizure and administration of "failed" firms. To be effective, regulators will somehow need to have better judgment and foresight in an always uncertain future than was in evidence during the last decade.

Along with the reliance on discretion come low transparency and few checks on errors or abuses of authority. The agencies are supposed to make "findings" to support their actions, but there is no opportunity for meaningful judicial review and legal accountability. Bailouts of the failed *firm* (that is, its stockholders) are prohibited, but bailouts of creditors are not; there is discretion over the allocation of losses among creditors. Ironically, proponents of Dodd-Frank always refer to its resolution procedure as "orderly," unlike bankruptcy resolution, which is always referred to as "disorderly," although in what respect is not elucidated. In reality, both procedures are highly structured, albeit along different lines and with different degrees of predictability.

All of this produces uncertainty and the associated costs to financial institutions and transactions. The role of market discipline by informed counterparties with financial stakes is diminished.

B. Chapter 14

There is less reliance on unexplained agency decisions reached in private and more on judicial hearings and reasoned public opinions. Greater emphasis is placed on preserving or creating private incentives to monitor and check firms accepting risks that outsiders view as excessive or misinformed.

Failure losses are allocated to creditors based on known claim priorities. It is true that a government can always intervene—if believed justified on economic (or political) grounds—to protect chosen creditors, for example, by acquiring or guaranteeing their claims and thus bearing their losses. But the action becomes transparent, may require congressional authorization, and is open to electoral accountability.

C. Policy Choices

1. Repeal Dodd-Frank, but such a turnaround seems politically unlikely. Or Title II could be extensively amended—conceivable, but complicated.
2. Enactment along the lines of Chapter 14 of an alternative resolution process.
   a. For a case of voluntary bankruptcy: Management would have an opportunity to take early reorganization action, including "prepackaged" filings, under a new chapter drafted for a SIFI's use.
   b. In a case of involuntary bankruptcy: The primary regulator could be required to justify to a district court (in a real, if closed, hearing with a rapid—but realistic—timetable for opposition and decision) its preference for an FDIC receivership. Even without enacting such a legally binding requirement, a rejection of the new alternative would at least have to be explained in the agency's recommendation and the Treasury Secretary's determination to seize the firm under Title II of the Act,[40] and therefore might make resort to that action less

---

40. §§ 203(a)(2)(F), 203(b)(2).

automatic. And the detailed "living wills" that all SIFIs have to design for a Bankruptcy Code resolution would become directly relevant, facilitating reorganizations.

3. Do nothing: Leave Title II of the Act as it is, assume it is not unconstitutional, and just hope it never has to be used. But its mere existence would continue to produce uncertainty and related costs. And an opportunity to make bankruptcy law a more effective and efficient alternative would have been lost.

2

Bankruptcy Code Chapter 14

A Proposal

Thomas H. Jackson

CONTENTS

INTRODUCTION

This chapter describes several proposed changes to the Bankruptcy Code that are designed for—and limited to—the reorganization or liquidation of the nation's largest financial institutions. The proposed changes create a new Chapter 14 of the Bankruptcy Code and incorporate features of liquidations under Chapter 7 as well as reorganizations under Chapter 11. In addition, the proposed Chapter 14 contains a number of substantive and procedural changes designed especially for the complexity, and potential systemic consequences, of the failure of these large financial institutions. We, the members of the Resolution Project group, believe it is possible through these changes to take advantage of a judicial proceeding—including explicit rules, designated in advance and honed through published judicial precedent, with appeals challenging the application of those rules, public proceedings, and transparency—in such a way as to minimize the felt necessity to use the alternative government agency resolution process recently enacted as a part of the Dodd-Frank Wall Street Reform and Consumer Protection Act. The new chapter could be adopted either in addition or as an alternative to the new resolution regime of Dodd-Frank.

The crucial feature of this new Chapter 14 is to ensure that the covered financial institutions, creditors dealing with them, and other market participants know in advance, in a clear and predictable way, how losses will be allocated if the institution fails. If the creditors of a failed financial institution are protected (bailed out), then the strongest and most rapidly responding constraint on risk taking by the financial institution's management is destroyed, and their losses are transferred to others.

In the following sections, we explain the features of this new Chapter 14 by **(a)** outlining existing bankruptcy provisions that we propose to amend or replace, **(b)** summarizing perceived weaknesses in those provisions that this proposal addresses, and **(c)** outlining the nature of the statutory provisions that are designed to address these weaknesses. These statutory changes can be encompassed within four basic categories: (1) the creation of a new Chapter 14, (2) the commencement of a Chapter 14 case, (3) the role of the primary regulator in Chapter 14 and special rules regarding debtor-in-possession financing for purposes of "prepayments" to certain creditors, and (4) the treatment of qualified financial contracts in Chapter 14. Following that, we provide in summary form a list of the changes we propose and the likely place in either the Bankruptcy Code or in Title 28 (the jurisdictional title) to make those changes.

I. CREATION OF A NEW CHAPTER 14

A. Define Financial Institution

1. Current Law
   There is no special definition of a financial institution.

2. Concerns
   Bankruptcy seems to be undervalued as a potential solution to the liquidation or reorganization of complex financial institutions, including in the 2010 congressional debate over financial reform, in part because of a view that the default of one or more of the nation's largest and most complex financial institutions is **(a)** outside the competence of the bankruptcy system, **(b)** unable to be resolved in a timely fashion in a judicial proceeding, and **(c)** likely to have systemic consequences that an adversarial system, which depends on

parties-in-interest with standing before the court, is ill-equipped to respond to.

3. Proposal

In order to craft a bankruptcy process that is responsive to the special needs of the nation's largest financial institutions, it is necessary to create a special set of procedures and rules for them. This starts, most fundamentally, with a need to provide a definition in the Bankruptcy Code of which financial institutions would be covered by these special procedures and rules. Because many of the concerns focus on the nation's largest institutions, with no strong sense that existing procedures are insufficient for other financial institutions, the definition should not only define what a "financial institution" is but should also set a threshold for the size of the institution before invoking the special rules and procedures we propose. The definition we recommend would define a "financial institution" for bankruptcy (and hence Chapter 14) purposes as an institution "that is substantially engaged in providing financial services or financial products," and includes "any subsidiaries of any such institution."[1] To eliminate purely "local" financial institutions, the definition would include a minimum asset size of $100 billion for the combined enterprise—a figure that should have a mechanism for adjustment with changes in the financial system.[2]

---

1. The Bankruptcy Code would use the word "person," which is defined in § 101(41) as including an "individual, partnership, and corporation." For convenience, this chapter often uses the word "institution."

2. Unlike Title II of Dodd-Frank, where a "covered financial company" can be determined after the fact (the category includes both firms that derive 85 percent of their revenues from activities that are financial in nature as well as any financial company designated as systemically important through an elaborate executive branch determination regarding systemic consequences), we propose using a predetermined size threshold, so as to remove uncertainty in terms of whether a particular institution

B. Create Chapter 14

1. Current Law
   No such chapter exists.

2. Concern
   Because of the special procedural and substantive rules that are perceived to be needed to make bankruptcy a robust alternative to government agency resolution for the nation's largest financial institutions, there needs to be a mechanism within the Bankruptcy Code for **(a)** incorporating the vast majority of common Bankruptcy Code provisions in Chapters 1 (general provisions), 3 (case administration and administrative powers [such as the automatic stay; the use, sale, or lease of property; obtaining credit; and the treatment of executory contracts]), and 5 (determining assets and claims, priorities, and provisions such as setoffs, and the recovery of preferences and fraudulent conveyances), as well as the "outcome" Chapters 7 (liquidation) and 11 (reorganization), while **(b)** ensuring that those special procedural and substantive rules for covered financial institutions govern and amend or override certain common Bankruptcy Code provisions.

3. Proposal
   In essence, our proposal provides a new bankruptcy process (including certain new substantive rules) for financial institutions for the liquidation or reorganization of these defined financial institutions. At the same time, the Bankruptcy Code's structure and rules for a liquidation proceeding, in Chapter 7, and for a reorganization

---

(on either a voluntary or involuntary petition) is appropriate for our proposed Chapter 14.

proceeding, in Chapter 11, provide a solid starting place, with a wealth of important judicial gloss on statutory terminology that would be usefully applied in many situations involving a covered financial institution. To accomplish both goals simultaneously, we propose that the proceeding (or "case") when a covered financial institution invokes (or is placed in) bankruptcy follow the rules of the existing Bankruptcy Code, *except* where we propose to change those rules. Particularly because our proposal envisions a different judicial "path," as we describe later (involving district judges in lieu of bankruptcy judges), to use the existing Bankruptcy Code structure and attempt to amend various provisions in Chapters 7 and 11 to accommodate our proposal would be cumbersome. Thus, our proposal is to create a new Chapter 14 in the Bankruptcy Code and require covered financial institutions to *concurrently* file for Chapter 14 *and* Chapter 7 or Chapter 11 (that is, covered financial institutions cannot file for Chapter 7 or Chapter 11 without also filing for Chapter 14), and requiring the resulting liquidation (Chapter 7) or reorganization (Chapter 11) proceeding to be conducted according to the rules and under the special court supervision of Chapter 14.

The essence of this change, then, would be to insert a new subsection into § 109,[3] which **(a)** limits Chapter 14 to financial institutions (as defined), **(b)** provides that a financial institution "may not be a debtor under Chapter 7 or Chapter 11 without first (or concurrently) commencing a case under Chapter 14," and **(c)** provides that all proceedings under this simultaneous Chapter 7 or Chapter 11 "shall be conducted pursuant to the provisions of Chapter 14."

---

3. All section numbers, unless explicitly indicated otherwise, refer to Title 11, U.S. Code.

C. Assign Chapter 14 Cases and Proceedings to Designated Article III District Judges

1. Current Law

    a. Judges. Because bankruptcy judges are not "Article III" judges (primarily because they do not enjoy lifetime tenure, which is a constitutional requirement for Article III judges), the Supreme Court, in *Northern Pipeline Construction Co. v. Marathon Pipe Line Co.*, 458 U.S. 50 (1982), struck down certain features of the original jurisdictional grant in the Bankruptcy Code of 1978 to bankruptcy judges to hear and decide various cases and controversies that arise in connection with bankruptcy proceedings. In response to *Northern Pipeline*, Congress enacted the current jurisdictional structure in 28 U.S.C. § 157. It provides that bankruptcy cases are "filed" in the district court (comprised of Article III judges), but that a district court may provide (as all have) that "cases under title 11 [the Bankruptcy Code]" and "proceedings arising under title 11," "shall be referred to the bankruptcy judges for the district." Those judges may then hear "cases under title 11" and "core proceedings arising under title 11," with 28 U.S.C. § 157(b)(2) attempting to define "core proceedings" in a way that is consistent with what the Supreme Court, in *Northern Pipeline*, said that non–Article III judges could "hear and determine." Things that are not core proceedings but are otherwise related to a bankruptcy case can be heard by a bankruptcy judge, but that judge can only "submit proposed findings of fact and conclusions of law to the district court," and the district court must issue "any final order or judgment," 28 U.S.C. § 157(c)(1).

    b. Venue. Bankruptcy cases can be commenced in the district court for the district that is the debtor's domicile: Its "principal place of business in the United States," where the "principal assets [of the debtor] in the United States are located," or in which an affiliate of the debtor has already filed, 28 U.S.C. § 1408, although cases can be transferred by a district court to another district "in the interest of justice or for the convenience of the parties," 28 U.S.C. § 1412.

2. Concerns

The current system ultimately depends on venue, and within venue, essentially random assignment of cases to bankruptcy judges for the district in which the bankruptcy case has been filed. While this is appropriate for the vast majority of business (and individual) bankruptcy cases that numerically dominate the system, it is unlikely that the nation's several hundred bankruptcy judges—all of whom can be presumed to have important knowledge of the Bankruptcy Code itself—will have the requisite financial expertise to deal, in real time, with the nation's largest financial institutions. To be sure, these institutions are clustered in a few venues, and one could envision (similar to our proposal) a designated panel of bankruptcy judges with requisite expertise, but there is a second concern as well that leads us to make a different proposal. In addition to the question of financial mastery necessary for complex financial institutions, the general bankruptcy procedure of automatically delegating bankruptcy cases from the district court to a bankruptcy court places the cases before non–Article III judges. While this is not troubling in the vast majority of bankruptcy cases, the essential need for complete independence from any perception of influence by the financial institution, the government, or a particularly significant creditor suggests that any bankruptcy system designed for the nation's largest financial institutions would want those institutions to have their cases and ancillary proceedings heard before an

Article III judge. In our system, there is no more "gold-plated" standard of independence from government.[4]

3. Proposal

Given the limited number of covered financial institutions, and the even more limited number that will be in bankruptcy at any given time, there is considerable merit to "funneling" such cases before a limited set of preselected Article III district judges. Our proposal is to funnel cases to the Second and DC Circuits, where a panel of district court judges has been predesignated to oversee Chapter 14 cases by the chief justice of the United States. These designated district judges would then have the same (and, to that extent, exclusive) jurisdiction over Chapter 14 cases that district judges currently have over other bankruptcy cases. These judges would be precluded from referring cases and proceedings to bankruptcy judges pursuant to 28 U.S.C. § 157(a), but they would have the power, by amendment to Title 28, to appoint a special master from a predesignated panel of special masters to hear the case and all proceedings under the case that could be heard by a bankruptcy judge. In addition, the district judge could similarly designate a bankruptcy judge, as well as experts, to provide necessary advice and input to the district judge or to the special master.

---

4. In *The Going-Concern Value of a Failed SIFI* (chapter 6 in this volume), Kenneth E. Scott and Thomas H. Jackson discuss more fully the advantages and limitations of Article III status through the lens of Chrysler's bankruptcy, which we believe was an abuse of the absolute priority rule of bankruptcy, in part through a "rigged" sale of most of Chrysler's assets under § 363, driven by the government. For present purposes, our point is that while no system can eliminate various government pressures on players and participants, an Article III judge is the least likely to "bend" the rules of the bankruptcy process to facilitate governmental favoritism or political forces.

II. COMMENCING A CHAPTER 14 CASE

A. Allow the Entire Covered Financial Institution (Including Subsidiaries) to Be Resolved in Bankruptcy

1. Current Law

While most entities with a place of business or property in the United States are eligible for bankruptcy, there are exclusions for:

- a domestic insurance company, § 109(b)(2), or a foreign insurance company engaged in business in the United States, § 109(b)(3)(A);
- a bank, savings bank, cooperative bank, savings and loan association, credit union, or similar entity "which is an insured bank as defined in section 3(h) of the Federal Deposit Insurance Act" (collectively, consider these "depository banks");
- a foreign bank, savings bank, cooperative bank, savings and loan association, credit union, or similar entity with a branch or agency (as defined in section 1(b) of the International Banking Act of 1978) in the United States.

In addition, there is an exclusion from eligibility for Chapter 11 (reorganization) but not for Chapter 7 for stockbroker and commodity brokers, § 109(d), as defined in §§ 101(6) and 101(53A). In essence, this forces stockbrokers and commodity brokers into special subchapters of Chapter 7. The important part of the stockbroker subchapter is that the Chapter 7 proceeding can be stayed, and then dismissed, upon the filing of "an application for a protective decree under the Securities Investor Protection Act of 1970." ("If SIPC [Securities Investor Protection Corporation] completes the liquidation of the debtor, then the court shall dismiss the case.") For commodity brokers, the Commodity Futures Trading Commission (CFTC) is given a right to be heard, § 762(b), and there are special rules for treating customer accounts "separately," §§ 763 and 766. (There is also a subchapter, commencing with § 781, for the liquidation of clearing banks, which makes the Federal Reserve Board (FRB)–designated conservator or receiver the trustee and provides for various methods for the "disposition" of the clearing bank.)

2. Concerns

Large financial institutions are oftentimes structurally complex and operate subsidiaries in a number of different areas, including those that are excluded from bankruptcy or are shunted to a special bankruptcy procedure. While the exclusion of depository banks has worked reasonably well for special reasons intimately related to the nature of the guaranteed deposit system, other exclusions, such as those for insurance companies, designed to leave their insolvency to state insurance agencies, never achieved that level of agreement or success and seem strangely disconnected with the broad scope of modern, large-scale insurance companies. Whatever their intent, these exclusions and special rules significantly complicate the resolution of a major financial institution, in which bankruptcy is only able to deal with pieces of the (often-integrated) whole and needs to coordinate, sometimes in awkward fashion, with nonbankruptcy resolution authorities that also have only a piece of the whole to work with.

3. Proposal

The Bankruptcy Code would be amended to:

- eliminate the exclusion in § 109(b)(2) and (b)(3)(A) for domestic and foreign insurance companies when Chapter 14 applies, but provide for treatment—to the extent consistent with the broader bankruptcy process for the covered financial institution—of insurance subsidiaries (and those they insure) with nonbankruptcy resolution processes;

- eliminate the exclusion of stockbrokers and commodity brokers from Chapter 11 when Chapter 14 applies by revising § 109(d). In doing this, the special subchapters for stockbrokers (§§ 741 et seq.) and commodity brokers (§§ 761 et seq.) in Chapter 7 would also be eliminated when Chapter 14 applies. The kinds of rules currently existing for the treatment of customer accounts in the commodity broker subchapter (particularly §§ 763 and 766) would be generalized and made applicable to bankruptcy proceedings (whether liquidations or reorganizations) of stockbrokers and commodity brokers, and the SIPC (for stockbrokers) or the CFTC (for commodity brokers) would be given a right to be a party to the proceeding.

The proposal does not change the current resolution practice of the Federal Deposit Insurance Corporation (FDIC) over depository banks.

B. Give the Primary Regulator the Power to File an Involuntary Petition

1. Current Law

There is no limitation on the commencement of a "voluntary" case—that is, a case begun by the filing of a petition by the debtor, § 301(a). "The commencement of a voluntary case under a chapter of this title constitutes an order of relief under such chapter," § 303(b).

Involuntary cases can be "commenced" by the filing by three or more creditors (some largely irrelevant exceptions exist), § 303(b).

2. Concern

Bankruptcy responds to the parties in a direct relationship with the debtor, such as creditors. Again, while this is appropriate for the vast majority of firms, financial or otherwise, there is a legitimate concern for the nation's largest financial institutions that "systemic" consequences going far beyond those direct relationships and affecting the functioning of the financial system need to be addressed as well.

3. Proposal

The existing provisions for the commencement of voluntary and involuntary cases would remain in place. There would be added to these provisions, by amending § 303(b) and (h), the ability of the primary regulator to commence an involuntary case against a financial institution for the same reasons as currently exist for three or more creditors.

C. Allow the Primary Regulator to File Based on "Balance Sheet" Insolvency

1. Current Law

If an involuntary case is contested, there is a "trial," and the court "shall order relief against the debtor" only if **(a)** "the debtor is generally not paying such debtor's debts as such debts become due" (unless the debts are subject to a bona fide dispute), § 303(h)(1), or **(b)** a custodian had been appointed or took possession within 120 days of the date of the filing of the petition, § 303(h)(2).

2. Concern

The Bankruptcy Code eliminated various forms of "balance sheet" insolvency as grounds for the commencement of an involuntary case, believing them (among other reasons) to be too subjective. While that concern has some validity, we believe that it is outweighed in cases of major financial institutions. In those cases, where there is a special concern of a financial "meltdown" leading to possible systemic consequences, limiting involuntary petitions to situations where the debtor is already failing to pay debts as they become due may be woefully late.

3. Proposal

Amend § 303(h) to provide that the primary regulator would be given the power to commence an involuntary case against a financial institution on the ground that either the financial institution's assets are less than its liabilities, at fair valuation, or the financial institution has an unreasonably small capital.[5] The financial institution could contest this (as it can any involuntary petition), although the likelihood is small that the filing would not, in essence, create a self-fulfilling prophesy.[6]

---

5. Since this is a change from the ordinary involuntary petition rules, added particularly because of a concern about systemic consequences, we have limited this expansion to the primary regulator, not to three or more creditors. If the "balance sheet" insolvency test for involuntary bankruptcy filings was to include unsecured creditors as petitioners, we would suggest a substantially higher aggregate threshold than the current $14,425 amount in Bankruptcy Code § 303(b).

6. Even without this power, it is probably the case that the primary regulator has many ways of "forcing" a weak financial institution to file a voluntary petition. Even so, it is important to make the regulator's power de jure as well as de facto, and this is the cleanest way to do that.

III. ROLE OF THE PRIMARY REGULATOR
IN CHAPTER 14; DIP FUNDING

A. Regulator Standing

1. Current Law

There is no provision for such standing, apart from the situation of stockbrokers and commodity brokers in Chapter 7.

2. Concern

Under the current system, certain parts of a complex financial institution cannot be resolved in bankruptcy. The regulators, instead, are tasked with the responsibility of dealing with financial distress for those parts outside of the bankruptcy process. This approach is needlessly complex and fraught with territorial conflicts and disputes, as compared with a framework that encompasses the liquidation or reorganization of a covered financial institution "in total" in bankruptcy. But to gain those advantages, it is important not to lose the expertise and perspective of the primary regulators.

3. Proposal

The regulators of the business of a covered financial institution, or any subsidiary thereof, would have standing with respect to the financial institution or the particular subsidiary, to be heard as parties or to raise motions relevant to their regulation with the Chapter 14 court.

B. Motions for the Use, Sale, or Lease of Property

1. Current Law

Under § 363, motions to use, sell, or lease property of the estate (except in the ordinary course of business) are to be filed by the trustee (or, pursuant to § 1107, the debtor-in-possession).

2. Concern

Because of the importance of preventing systemic consequences, there may be situations in which the government is the only appropriate party to determine that the use, sale, or lease of property of the estate is important and proper; even so, the government's determination must be subject to court review to ensure that it is not likely to harm or favor certain creditors of the financial institution that is in bankruptcy.

3. Proposal

Section 363 should be amended to provide that the primary regulator has the power, in parallel with the trustee or debtor-in-possession, to file motions for the use, sale, or lease of property of the estate. As is currently the case, approval of such a motion would be subject to the safeguards provided in § 363.

C. Debtor-in-Possession (DIP) Financing

1. Current Law

If the business is continuing in operation (which is the ordinary course in Chapter 11, but is also plausibly involved in a Chapter 7 for at least a while), the debtor-in-possession, § 1107(a), or a trustee appointed in lieu of a debtor-in-possession, § 1108, is authorized to obtain unsecured credit and incur unsecured debt, in the ordinary course of business (and without court approval), with such credit/debt having "administrative expense" priority, § 364(a). (Administrative expense priorities are the expenses of running the bankruptcy proceeding, which [simplifying somewhat] essentially rank *before* prebankruptcy unsecured claims but *after* prebankruptcy secured claims in priority, §§ 507(a)(2), 725, and 726.) Under § 364(b), administrative expense priority can also be given to other funding that does not qualify as being in the "ordinary course of business," but now only upon court approval, after notice and a hearing. If administrative expense priority is insufficient to obtain credit, the court becomes involved and priority can be increased, subject to increasingly rigorous requirements. It may be authorized, after notice and a hearing: **(a)** with priority over other administrative expenses, or with a security interest on property that is not already subject to a security interest, or with a junior security interest on property that is already subject to a security interest, § 364(c); or **(b)** with a senior or equal security interest on property already subject to a security interest, however, the court must now find not only that the financing is not otherwise available but also that the existing secured creditors receive "adequate protection" under § 361 of their security interest, § 364(d). (The latter is very difficult to establish, because it basically requires a showing that no one is willing to lend without priority over (or parity with) an existing secured credit *and* the debtor can demonstrate that the existing secured creditor is no worse off than it was before.)

2. Concerns

There may be situations where liquidity or other systemic concerns suggest that the appropriate action—without involving a government bailout of any sort—would be for certain liquidity-sensitive creditors to be "advanced" a portion of their likely bankruptcy distribution, which would be accomplished through DIP financing. It is unlikely that § 364, which focuses on funding ongoing operations, not prepayments to existing creditors, currently would allow such as result. Because of the necessity of an estimation of final distribution, this possibility needs to be carefully circumscribed, however.

Because of the importance of the principle, it is perhaps worth outlining the concern with a numerical example. Assume the debtor has assets of $100 million and unsecured claims of $300 million. Without any prepayments, the expected distribution at the end of the bankruptcy proceeding would be 33 cents on the dollar to the unsecured creditors. If, however, there is a determination that the "liquidity-sensitive (LS) creditors" with unsecured claims of $100 million should receive advanced payments, and those advanced payments come from funding under § 364, the problem of "aggressive" prepayment manifests itself in this way. Assume that the debtor (or the government) persuades the court that a "conservative" payout to the LS creditors would be $50 million (or 50 cents on the dollar), and the government will provide that funding pursuant to § 364. The following changes occur: **(a)** the LS creditors receive $50 million (instead of $33 ⅓ million), and **(b)** the government has an administrative expense (or higher-priority) claim for $50 million, § 364(b). Because of these two changes, the debtor still has assets of $100 million (the government's money came and went, leaving the assets as before), but now has an administrative expense claim (held by the government) of $50 million and $200 million of remaining unsecured claims (i.e., claims that did not receive an advance payment). Following ordinary bankruptcy distribution rules, the government would get the first $50 million of the debtor's assets, leaving $50 million for the remaining $200 million of unsecured creditors. In short, because of the "aggressive" prepayment, the LS creditors receive a distribution of 50 cents on the dollar rather than 33 cents on the dollar, and the remaining unsecured creditors receive a distribution of 25 cents on the dollar, rather than 33 cents on the dollar. The LS creditors are better off and the remaining creditors are worse off. The government is, financially, indifferent, but it has—through this—accomplished a partial bailout of the LS creditors. The innocent parties (beyond the taxpayers) in this are the remaining unsecured creditors, whose share of the bankruptcy estate went from 33 cents on the dollar to 25 cents on the dollar. To undo this, it is necessary either to "claw back" the difference between 33 and 50 cents on the dollar from the LS creditors or to require the government's $50 million claim to be subordinated to the remaining unsecured creditors to the tune of $16⅔ million (one-third of the total)—so the government would receive $33⅓ million, and there would be $66⅔ million left for distribution to the remaining $200 million of unsecured creditors. (While this has focused on the government as funder, because the innocent "victims" are the remaining unsecured creditors, a similar concern would arise even if the $50 million funding to the LS creditors came from a private source.)

3. Proposal

The proposal would add a provision making it clear that DIP financing is available in Chapter 14 pursuant to § 364(b) (nonordinary-course financing, as well as § 364(c) and (d))—all of which require court approval after notice and a hearing—for financing that will permit partial or complete payouts to some or all creditors where liquidity of those creditors is a concern, and the payments are intended as "advances" for the likely payouts such creditors would receive in a liquidation or a reorganization at the end of the bankruptcy process. To prevent unfair treatment of creditors entitled to particular distributions under the Bankruptcy Code, approval of any such request would be subject to several burden of proof requirements. First, the movant would be required to show the necessity (for liquidity or other systemic reasons) of the payout (including its amount) to particular creditors.[7] Second, the movant would be

---

7. Any creditors receiving such advanced payout, at least in the case of a reorganization, would necessarily constitute a separate "class" under § 1122(a) for purposes of voting on the plan.

required to show that such payout is less than a conservative estimate of the amount those creditors would receive in bankruptcy without such prepayment. Third (and logically following from the second), the movant would be required to show that any such prepayment was not likely to favor particular creditors or classes of creditors, or otherwise undermine the operation of the absolute priority rule embodied in §§ 725 and 726, and the plan confirmation requirements of § 1129. If the government is the entity providing the funding, it will additionally be required to show that no private funding on reasonably comparable terms is available. Those provisions on burden of proof should be written into the statute, in an analogous fashion to the burden of proof on issues of adequate protection of secured creditors in § 364(d)(2).

In addition, it shall be a provision of any such funding that, should the payout exceed the amount that the creditors would have received in the bankruptcy proceeding in the absence of such funding, the entity providing the funding, in clear and explicit fashion, agrees to subordinate its § 364 funding claim to the claims of the remaining creditors to the extent of that excess.

D. Filing Plans of Reorganization

1. Current Law

In Chapter 11, the debtor may file a plan at any time, including at the time of its voluntary petition (a "prepack"), § 1121(a). Any other party in interest (including a creditor or a creditor's committee), can usually file a plan (there are a couple of largely unimportant exceptions) only if the debtor has not filed a plan within the first 120 days, § 1121(c)(2), unless, upon request and after notice and hearing, the court reduces (or increases) that period (which is known as the debtor's "exclusivity" period).

2. Concerns

Given the concerns with systemic consequences, as well as speed, a presumptive 120-day exclusivity period for plan formulation and filing given to the debtor-in-possession (i.e., existing management, usually selected by the former shareholders, who are now presumably "out of the money") is cumbersome and potentially destructive of significant value that depends on rapid resolution.

3. Proposal

In addition to the debtor, in the case of a Chapter 14 proceeding, allow the primary regulator or a creditors' committee to file a plan of reorganization at any time after the order for relief (which occurs upon filing in a voluntary case, § 301(b), and after a court order in the case of a contested involuntary petition, § 303(h)). This would be accomplished either through an amendment to § 1121 ("Who may file a plan") or through a provision in Chapter 14 that provided "notwithstanding § 1121(c)," the entities listed previously could file a plan of reorganization at any time after the order for relief.

IV. QUALIFIED FINANCIAL CONTRACTS IN CHAPTER 14

Introduction

The current—like our proposed—treatment of various forms of qualified financial contracts (QFCs) is complex and easily misunderstood. In essence, our proposal has three major parts, two of which focus on the automatic stay and one that focuses on the trustee's avoiding powers (preference law, in particular).[8] The first part, which concerns repos, proposes modest changes in current bankruptcy law, mostly to clarify that, for purposes of Chapter 14 (and hence for covered financial institutions), the automatic stay does not apply to repos (which will be treated as a form of secured loans that are automatically "breached" by the debtor upon the commencement of a bankruptcy case) in terms of netting, setoff, or collateral sales by the counterparty of cashlike collateral that is in its possession. The second part, which concerns derivatives, proposes short-term, more-significant changes in current bankruptcy law. For three days, the counterparty will be subject to bankruptcy's automatic stay and therefore stayed from exercising any right under an ipso facto clause (unless the debtor first explicitly rejects the derivative contract) to enable the debtor to exercise its choice between assumption and rejection of this form of executory contract. After three days, and unless the debtor has previously assumed the derivative, the counterparty will be free to exercise any rights it may have under ipso facto clauses (or otherwise) to terminate the derivative and, upon termination (either by action of the counterparty or by rejection by the debtor), the counterparty will have the netting, setoff, and collateral sale rights of a repo counterparty in bankruptcy. The third part, which concerns both repos and derivatives, applies trustee's avoiding powers, including preference law, to

---

8. While our focus is on QFCs in Chapter 14, we believe that these changes are not tied in any specific way to financial institutions covered by Chapter 14. Thus, in our view, it would be desirable to incorporate these proposals so as to be applicable to any bankruptcy proceeding, whether or not dealing with a covered financial institution in Chapter 14. For a fuller analysis of these issues, *see* both Darrell Duffie and David Skeel's contribution to this volume (chapter 5), as well as David Skeel & Thomas Jackson, *Transaction Consistency and the New Finance in Bankruptcy*, 112 Colum. L. Rev. 152 (2012).

such transactions, but also provides a "two-point net improvement test" safe harbor for certain payments and collateral transfers that otherwise would be subject to preference attack. These three parts are only briefly summarized here; a more detailed consideration of each—such as provisions dealing with the sale of other types of collateral or the enforceability of master agreements—is developed later in this chapter.

A. Repos and the Automatic Stay

1. Background

Before looking at current law, or at the proposal, it is useful to have some background information about the treatment of loans in bankruptcy, and the likely treatment of repos under normal bankruptcy rules (rather than the special rules that have been added governing their treatment).

Loans—situations where a creditor has loaned money to a debtor and awaits a repayment—are considered "claims" in bankruptcy of the debtor. The essence of a "claim" is that it is a liability from the perspective of the debtor. Since the debtor has already received the funds and the only obligation remaining is the debtor's repayment, it is a classic liability. The filing of a bankruptcy petition effectively "breaches" (or, to use language we will see later more precisely fits the terminology of the Bankruptcy Code, "rejects") this repayment obligation. This occurs automatically. The creditor does not need to take any action and the debtor is not permitted to "assume" the obligation. The claim is "accelerated" and valued as of the date of the filing of the petition; interest accruing after that date is disallowed unless the debtor has a security interest and is "oversecured." Thus, if the debtor borrowed $10,000 from the creditor on February 1 with repayment on June 1 and files for bankruptcy on April 1, the claim would be for $10,000 plus accrued but unpaid interest to that date.

The creditor is stopped by the essential nature of bankruptcy as a collective proceeding from taking any steps to collect this claim. The "automatic stay" of § 362 prohibits "any act to collect, assess, or recover a claim against the debtor that arose before the commencement of the case under this title," § 362(a)(6). This includes any setoff of a prepetition claim against a prepetition obligation that the debtor may owe the creditor, § 362(a)(8). (The *right* of setoff is recognized by bankruptcy law, § 553, but *exercising* it is prohibited by the automatic stay without first seeking court permission.)

If the loan is secured by collateral, the automatic stay extends to any effort to seize, use, or sell that collateral, § 362(a)(3), (4), (5); this would include collateral in the possession of the creditor. (Indeed, pursuant to § 542(a), the secured party may need to turn over the collateral to the debtor if it is the type of property that the debtor may "use, sell, or lease" under § 363.) The debtor is relieved of any obligation to post additional collateral. If there is a danger that the existing collateral will decline in value during the bankruptcy proceeding (traditionally because the debtor is using the collateral, but it would extend to market fluctuations as well), the secured creditor may ask the court for "adequate protection" of its security interest under § 361. Under a Supreme Court interpretation of the Bankruptcy Code, the secured party is not compensated for the delay itself—for the "time value" of money—unless the secured party's collateral is worth more than the amount of the loan outstanding.

In short, in the case of a secured loan, upon the filing of a petition in bankruptcy: **(a)** the loan is "breached" and valued as of that date; **(b)** the collateral is similarly valued as of that date and further decreases in its value are protected, upon request, by "adequate protection"; **(c)** the debtor is relieved of any obligation to post additional collateral; and **(d)** the secured creditor cannot take steps to collect the debt, including by self-help (setoff or selling collateral in its possession), without first getting bankruptcy court permission.

Most repos, despite their form (a sale and repurchase), are in fact considered by practitioners to be secured loans, and it is very probable that virtually all repos would be recharacterized to *be* secured loans by Article 9 of the Uniform Commercial Code. (Article 9 applies to "a transaction, *regardless of its form*, that creates a security interest in personal property," § 9–109(a)(1).)[9] Thus, their *probable* treatment in bankruptcy, apart from "special" rules, would likely be identical to what has been described earlier in terms of secured loans.

With this as background, we can turn to the current and proposed treatment of repos vis-à-vis the automatic stay in bankruptcy.

2. Current Law

Under § 559, a repo counterparty can terminate a repo notwithstanding a "condition" of the sort that is invalidated by § 365(e)(1). Unlike ordinary contract creditors, who cannot enforce so-called ipso facto clauses that allow termination at the event of the commencement of a bankruptcy case or the debtor's insolvency, repo counterparties are permitted to invoke these provisions, § 559. Under § 362(b)(7), a repo counterparty also can offset or net out obligations (including transfer obligations) under one or more repo agreements, including a master agreement, notwithstanding the automatic stay. (Although this language, added in 2006, is not crystal clear, it is apparent from prior language and intent that this includes the repo counterparty's ability to sell the "collateral" (the property that is the subject of the repo) that is in its—or its agent's—possession.)

---

9. Emphasis added.

3. Concerns

Current law suggests "special" treatment vis-à-vis the automatic stay for repos when, in fact, ordinary bankruptcy principles would lead to much the same result. At the same time, because of the complete exemption of current law, there is no attention paid to types of collateral. And, even with the special repo rules in bankruptcy, the right of a repo counterparty to marketable securities that are in the possession of the debtor, even upon motion, is unclear.

4. Proposal

Very little would change because of two overarching principles. First, as a matter of nonbankruptcy law, repos are forms of secured loans (see earlier discussion). Second, because the property that is the subject of repos is usually marketable securities or other cash-like instruments, there is no "firm-specific" value to the assets and there is little subjectivity regarding their market value. Putting together these two principles, the following emerges: First, repos are automatically breached upon the filing of a bankruptcy petition. Second, because all repos are breached, no such provision in a master agreement that cross-links repos is necessary to ensure that the breach of one is considered a ground to terminate all (since all have been terminated automatically upon the filing of a bankruptcy petition). Third, because of the highly marketable attributes of the property that is oftentimes the subject of repos—the "secured property" in the recharacterization of repos as secured loans—there is little reason to prohibit the sale of such property, if it is in the possession of the counterparty, by the automatic stay. Since all the repos are breached by the filing of the bankruptcy petition, the setting off or netting out across repos invades no bankruptcy norm and should also be allowed—although master agreements that allow netting of repos against derivatives or other qualified financial contracts would be limited to netting across repos. These results are all consistent with the current Bankruptcy Code "special rules" involving repos, and thus—despite their linguistic awkwardness—no change in either § 559 or § 362(b)(7) is necessary. The changes we propose are threefold:

First, our proposal would ensure that the right of collateral sales of repos by counterparties—without court permission and where the debtor is in bankruptcy—is limited to cashlike or otherwise highly marketable securities. (Arguments that the debtor "needs" access to the cashlike assets [by definition, in possession or control of the counterparty] conflates DIP financing, discussed earlier, with firm-specific collateral, which cashlike collateral is not. Requiring the counterparty to be a DIP financer, with "adequate protection" of its secured interest given in return, is both coercive and defaults to the highest level of DIP financing priority because of the requirement of providing the counterparty with adequate protection. The issue of DIP financing, which our Chapter 14 proposal addresses, should not be conflated with the idea that a secured creditor holding cash-like collateral should be able to sell it because it is neither **(a)** firm-specific nor **(b)** subject to valuation manipulations.) Precisely because of the lack of firm-specific value and the ease of valuation, our proposal is limited to cashlike or otherwise highly marketable securities. If a repo involved (for example) a drill press, that repo's counterparty would not be automatically exempted from the automatic stay (on selling the collateral).

Second, our proposal would give the repo counterparty the right to sell other, non–firm-specific collateral in its possession upon motion to the court and the court's determination of the collateral's reasonable value.

Third, for situations where the collateral is in the hands of the debtor, not the repo counterparty, we propose to amend § 362, for

Chapter 14 purposes, to give a right of relief upon petition by a counterparty seeking to sell collateral backing the repos in the possession of the debtor to the extent that collateral consists of highly marketable securities or other cashlike collateral (which can be easily valued and does not have firm-specific value) as well as other non–firm-specific collateral upon the court's determination of the collateral's reasonable value.

B. Derivatives/Swaps and the Automatic Stay

1. Background

Before turning to current law or our proposals, it is useful, as for repos, to discuss the background treatment of "executory contracts" in bankruptcy, and what the likely treatment of derivatives/swaps in bankruptcy would be vis-à-vis the automatic stay under normal bankruptcy rules.

Derivatives/swaps, analytically, come in two different (but closely related) forms. In one form, they set (or guarantee) a price on a certain date. As such, they are (as a matter of form) analogous to a contract entered into on February 1, for the debtor to buy widgets on June 1 for $1,000. A simple future or forward contract—such as a contract to buy oil at a specified price on June 1, takes this form. The second is a protection (such as against default or a price change) over time. An interest rate or currency swap is a familiar example, as are credit default swaps. As such, these contracts are analogous (as a matter of form) to a fire insurance policy on a building. As a matter of bankruptcy law, the widget contract is considered an "executory contract" under § 365, since it consists of materially unperformed obligations on both sides (the buyer needs to pay and the seller needs to deliver). The same would be true of an insurance contract where the debtor had not already paid for the insurance. The fundamental notion of an executory contract is that the debtor has a right to either "assume" (i.e., determine that the contract is a net asset) or "reject" (i.e., determine that the contract is a net liability). Upon assumption, the contract is treated as if it was one entered into by the debtor in bankruptcy, and thus the debtor is expected to perform, with any damages resulting from a failure to perform treated as an administrative expense claim rather than a prepetition claim. Upon assumption, the debtor must comply with the terms of the contract, including the posting of additional collateral (although the debtor may "assign" the contract to another party upon the provision of adequate assurance of performance by the assignee, notwithstanding contractual provisions prohibiting such assignment, § 365(f)). However, if the debtor decides that the contract is a net liability, the debtor may "reject" the contract, in which case, any resulting damage claim is treated as a prepetition claim whose value is determined as of the filing of bankruptcy, just as in the case of ordinary loans (or repos). This right of the debtor to choose between assumption and rejection cannot be circumvented by a term in the contract that permits the nondebtor party to terminate because of bankruptcy or the financial condition of the debtor. As discussed under repos, clauses that permit this are called "ipso facto" clauses in bankruptcy and are normally unenforceable; see § 365(e)(1). The effect of a termination by the nondebtor party pursuant to an ipso facto clause would be to remove the choice of the debtor to "assume" the contract—that is, determine (from the perspective of the bankruptcy estate) that the contract was a net asset. That is prohibited by bankruptcy, as is any setoff right or collateral disposition, because of the operation of the automatic stay, as discussed under repos.

In short, in the case of executory contracts, in bankruptcy (a) the debtor has a right to decide whether to "assume" or to "reject" the contract; **(b)** this right cannot be eliminated by any right of the other party to terminate based on an ipso facto clause; **(c)** the automatic stay applies during this interregnum to prohibit the other party from setting off, selling collateral, or otherwise attempting to collect on the underlying obligation; **(d)** if the debtor "rejects," then analytically the contract is treated in the same manner as a loan or repo, discussed previously; **(e)** if the debtor "assumes," then the contract is treated as one "created by" the debtor in bankruptcy, and thus one for which it needs to perform (including additional collateral postings); any breach of that obligation would be equivalent to a breach of a postpetition "administrative expense priority" contract; and **(f)** the debtor may, following assumption, "assign" the contract.

There is little doubt that, apart from the special provisions governing derivatives/swaps, they would be considered to be executory contracts, treated as are other executory contracts as described previously. With this as background, we can turn to the current and proposed treatment of swaps and derivatives vis-à-vis the automatic stay in bankruptcy.

2. Current Law

Here, unlike the case with respect to repos, the special rules for derivatives/swaps do, in fact, significantly change the rights of a derivative/swap counterparty in bankruptcy vis-à-vis the rights of an ordinary secured creditor. Section 560 calls off the application of § 365(e)(1)—and thus permits the counterparty to terminate based on an ipso facto clause. The effect of a termination by the counterparty pursuant to an ipso facto clause is to remove the choice of the debtor to "assume" the contract. And, upon termination, a parallel exception built into § 362(b)(17) allows the counterparty "to offset or net out any termination value, payment amount, or other transfer obligation arising under or in connection with 1 or more such agreements." This permits "self-help" by the counterparty, including selling any collateral that might be in its possession. [If the collateral is not in its possession, there is no comparable exception to the automatic stay that would allow the counterparty to pursue collateral in the possession of the debtor without first gaining court permission, so that is not an issue.] Because of the master agreement provisions, any rejection or termination of any one derivative/swap with a counterparty is grounds for the counterparty's termination of all the derivatives within the same master agreement, thus precluding the debtor "cherry-picking" which derivatives/swaps with a counterparty to assume (because a net asset) or reject (because a net liability). A provision determining that "breach of one is a ground for the termination of all" is enforceable.

The provisions do seem to require the counterparty, in order to terminate, to take some concrete step toward that (such as notifying the debtor that it is terminating the contract). In the interim, the debtor remains free to assume or reject under § 365. (Indeed, *Metavante* suggests that unless the counterparty terminates a derivative/swap in a rather quick time frame, it loses the right to avoid assumption under § 365 by the debtor.)[10]

3. Concerns

By removing derivatives completely from the automatic stay, a debtor may be precluded from assuming valuable derivatives (subject to a master agreement that may, functionally, require an "all-or-nothing" determination). Both the FDIC resolution model for depository banks and the recently enacted government agency

---

10. *In re Lehman Brothers Holdings Inc.*, Case 08-13555 (Bankruptcy SDNY Sept. 15, 2009), more commonly known as the *Metavante* case.

resolution procedures for financial institutions under the Dodd-Frank Act provide a one-day window in which the debtor (or the government agency) may decide to assume and assign derivatives that place bankruptcy in a significant disadvantage (from the perspective of the financial institution) as an alternative.

4. Proposal

Although the debtor should be on a tight time leash with respect to the decision whether to assume or reject, the fundamental nature of derivatives/swaps as forms of executory contracts suggests that the debtor should have the right to determine whether to assume or to reject them. This means that during this period, the counterparty should be subject to the automatic stay, as well as precluded from terminating any derivative/swap because of an ipso facto clause. At the same time, whether as a matter of a "vested" provision of a master agreement (that cannot be undone by the debtor rejecting the master agreement itself) or the consequences of a right of setoff that is not excluded from the stay, the counterparty should retain the right to terminate any or all derivatives/swaps with the debtor should the debtor decide to reject, under § 365, *any* derivative/swap with the counterparty. Because of that, the debtor cannot "cherry-pick"—picking the derivatives/swaps with a particular counterparty that it views as net assets, and assuming them, while rejecting all derivatives/swaps that it views as net liabilities. The interplay of the right of the debtor to assume or reject and the counterparty to treat the rejection of one as the rejection of all leads to a global decision of the debtor (vis-à-vis any single counterparty) to assume or reject all derivatives/swaps with that counterparty. In addition, should the debtor assume derivatives/swaps, the ordinary rules of § 365 should allow the debtor to assign those derivatives/

swaps as well, upon the provision of adequate assurance of performance by the assignee. (This is essential to allowing bankruptcy to have going-concern values of large financial institutions and mirrors, in that respect, the "bridge" institution ability of FDIC resolution and Title II of Dodd-Frank.)

With prebankruptcy planning and wind-down plans, and with recognition of the right (currently one that can be circumvented by a counterparty by the special QFC bankruptcy rules) of the debtor to decide whether to assume or reject, the automatic stay, as well as the normal rules prohibiting termination based on ipso facto clauses, should apply for a period of three days from the time of the filing of the bankruptcy petition. After that, the debtor's right to assume the derivatives/swaps can be terminated by the counterparty (pursuant to the agreement's termination provisions; until termination by the counterparty has occurred, the debtor continues to have the right to assume). Upon termination, the counterparty enjoys all the rights described previously under repos vis-à-vis setoff and collateral sales: for example, the right of collateral sales (without going to court) in the case of marketable securities and other cashlike collateral in the counterparty's possession, with both recognized market values and no firm-specific value; the right of collateral sales, upon motion, for other collateral without firm-specific value and upon court determination of the fair value of the collateral; and the right, upon motion, to access collateral of the categories just identified, still in the possession of the debtor.

There are concerns that no such short stay, such as our proposal of three days, could possibly allow a debtor to "net out" the value of potentially thousands of related swaps. Whether or not true under the existing procedures—and we note that an even more aggressive abbreviated timetable exists for depository banks under the FDIC resolution procedure and in Title II of Dodd-Frank—it is also the case that recent requirements, including Dodd-Frank's insistence on "living wills" as well as its push to have swaps traded on exchanges, will go far to make "net out" valuations much more instantaneous, and thus potentially consistent in terms of quick valuation and evaluation with the brief stay we favor.

Operationally, this would be accomplished through the following changes, applicable to Chapter 14, of current bankruptcy provisions. The single most important "fix" would be to condition the application of § 560 on the expiration of three days from the filing of a petition in bankruptcy by a financial institution.[11] Prior to the termination of that period, the derivative/swap counterparty (like a party to any other comparable executory contract) would not have the right to terminate the contract without going to court first. And the debtor would have, as it does with other comparable executory contracts, the right to decide to assume (and, if appropriate, assign) or reject the derivative contract (although a master agreement or the setoff right might make that exercise an "all-or-nothing" affair).

This change (i.e., the limitation that would be written into § 560) would mean that the counterparty could *not* offset, net out, or sell collateral unless and until **(a)** the debtor decides to reject the contract and it is (by that action) terminated, or **(b)** the three-day time period for the debtor to decide whether to assume or reject expires. Upon termination (either by the counterparty, upon the expiration of the three-day time period, or by the debtor when it

---

11. Although not the current focus (which is on derivatives/swaps), §§ 555 and 556, which deal with securities contracts and forward contracts in an analogous manner to § 560, should likewise be conditioned on the expiration of three days from the filing of a petition in bankruptcy by a financial institution.

rejects the contract), the existing § 362(b)(17) rights (which are opaquely worded and should be clarified) would remain—that is, a right to set off one contract against another without first going to court and, ancillary to that, sell collateral in the possession of the counterparty without first going to court. With the understanding, that should be made the basis of statutory distinction, that most of that collateral will be financial instruments—or cashlike collateral (with recognized market values)—the ability of a counterparty to "self-help" by selling collateral (in its possession) or netting out need not be a major disruption to the ongoing operations of the debtor and would not need to be repealed.

The right of a counterparty, under a master agreement, to "cross-link" derivatives/swaps so that the rejection of one by the debtor would permit the counterparty to treat all of the derivatives/swaps as terminated (thus precluding the debtor's assumption of any of them) would remain in force.[12] Section 362 should also be amended, for Chapter 14 purposes, to give a right of relief upon petition by a counterparty seeking to sell collateral backing the derivatives/swaps **(a)** in the possession of the counterparty that, while not highly marketable, has no firm-specific value upon the determination of its fair market value; **(b)** in the possession of the debtor to the extent that collateral consists of highly marketable securities or other cashlike collateral (which can be easily valued and does not have firm-specific value); and **(c)** in the possession of the debtor to the

---

12. This right, however, would be limited to cross-linking derivatives/swaps pursuant to a master agreement. The master agreement would not be enforceable to the extent it attempted to cross-link repos and derivatives/swaps. Since repos are automatically "terminated" upon the filing of a bankruptcy petition, cross-linking across these categories would allow a counterparty with one (small) repo to avoid the debtor's ability to assume all derivatives/swaps under § 365. The master agreement provisions in the Bankruptcy Code should be amended to make this clear.

extent that the collateral consists of other non–firm-specific collateral, upon the determination of its fair market value.

C. Repos, Derivatives/Swaps, and Trustee's Avoiding Powers

1. Background

Bankruptcy has several devices, usually lumped together under the rubric of "trustee's avoiding powers" to protect dismemberment of the estate, either through actions of the debtor or through actions of creditors to seek to protect themselves, after making a loan or entering into a contract, from the consequences of an imminent bankruptcy proceeding. The most important of these "reach back" avoiding powers are **(a)** fraudulent transfers, §548, and **(b)** preferences, §547.

Under § 548, the fraudulent transfer provision,[13] the trustee (or debtor-in-possession) may avoid two types of transfers as fraudulent: The first, in § 548(a)(1)(A), are transfers made within two years of bankruptcy "with actual intent to hinder, delay, or defraud any entity"—this is known as the actual fraud provision. The second, in § 548(a)(1)(B), known as the constructive fraud provision, reaches prebankruptcy transfers within two years of bankruptcy where the debtor "received less than a reasonably equivalent value" at a time when the debtor was insolvent, had unreasonably small capital, or believed that it would incur debts beyond its ability to pay.

Under § 547, the preference section, the trustee may avoid a transfer "on account of an antecedent debt," made within 90 days

---

13. The trustee also has access to state fraudulent transfer provisions pursuant to his § 544 "lien creditor" powers, which oftentimes have a longer reach-back period than the two-year period provided by § 548.

of bankruptcy and while the debtor was insolvent,[14] that enables a creditor to receive more than it would have received, in bankruptcy, had the transfer not been made. Thus, transfers are not just payments but would include things such as the posting of additional collateral on an existing contract ("on account of an antecedent debt"). There is an exception for transfers that are both intended and are in fact, "a contemporaneous exchange for new value given to the debtor," although it is essential to note that "new value" is defined as excluding "an obligation substituted for an existing obligation," § 547(a)(2). There is also, for security interests in inventory or receivables, what is known as a "two-point net improvement" test, which looks at whether "the aggregate of all such transfers caused a reduction," on the commencement of bankruptcy, of the creditor's claim 90 days before bankruptcy (or the date on which new value was first given), § 547(c)(5). (Thus, the fact that the inventory went down in value and then went back up in value would be ignored, unless the inventory value on the date of bankruptcy was greater than the inventory value 90 days before bankruptcy.)

2. Current Law

Under § 546(e), (f), (g), and (j), the trustee's avoiding powers (with the exception of the actual fraud provision of § 548) are not enforceable against the holder of qualified financial contracts. This started with what is now § 546(e), exempting the transfers of margin and settlement payments by or to brokers (an exemption that makes some sense since these payments usually do not have the

---

14. "Insolvent" is defined in § 101(32) as having debts greater than assets, at fair valuation. The period is extended from 90 days to one year if the transfer is made to or benefits an "insider" of the debtor.

hallmarks of "opt out" activity on the eve of bankruptcy). From this narrow beginning, the Bankruptcy Code has been amended to provide similar protection for *all* qualified financial contracts, including repos, § 546(f), and derivatives/swaps, § 546(g).

3. Concerns

QFC counterparties tend to be among the most sophisticated creditors of a financial institution. Providing a safe harbor from preference law (and other avoiding powers of the trustee), when "regular" creditors are subject to such powers, seems perverse in that it protects the parties most likely to "see" bankruptcy coming and take steps to protect themselves or, alternatively, take steps that lead to a bankruptcy case being commenced in a more timely fashion. While there are special features of various QFCs that do not fit comfortably into existing preference law, a blanket exemption seems overbroad.

4. Proposal

With respect to repos and derivatives/swaps, and subject to an amendment to § 547(c)(5) regarding an extension of a "two-point net improvement" safe harbor that is discussed subsequently, remove the current exemption from trustee's avoiding powers by amending § 546(f) and (g) (as well as § 546(j), which repeats the protection for transfers made pursuant to a master netting agreement) to provide that these provisions do not apply in a Chapter 14 proceeding.

It is important to understand what this does and what it does not do (here, focusing on the preference provisions of § 547). Because of the nature of preference law—did a creditor improve his position at the expense of other creditors via a transfer within the preference period?—"improvements in position" by a creditor that are due to market increases in value of collateral are *not* subject to preference attack. Say a security, posted as collateral, is worth $70,000 on 90 days before bankruptcy and is worth $90,000 at the time of bankruptcy. The $20,000 "improvement in position" is not a voidable preference because it involves no "transfer of property of the debtor" (and, conceptually, does not diminish the returns to the other creditors). Because of this feature and the nature of repos, most repos will not be subject to attack under § 547. With a typical repo in which the debtor promises to buy back property that had been previously sold to a counterparty, fluctuations in the value of that property due to market forces between the sale and repurchase are not preferences under § 547; recharacterizing the transaction as a secured loan does not change the underlying preference analysis. Preference law would matter in cases where notwithstanding the sale/repurchase form, the property subject to the repo declines in value and the repurchaser (the failed financial institution) posts additional property. Treated as a secured loan, this is equivalent to the posting of collateral with an original value of $70,000 that declines within the preference period to $60,000, leading to a requirement that the debtor post an additional $10,000 of collateral. Preference law would treat this additional posting as a voidable preference.

Preference law, however, looms larger for swaps and other derivatives, where collateral is in fact used to secure an underlying obligation. Here, however, it is still the case that increases in the value of collateral due to market forces are not themselves preferential. And there is a second, important situation in which "new" collateral would not be preferential, which we call "rollover" derivatives. To see this, consider the following reasoning. While the definition of "new value" in § 547(a)(2) excludes "an obligation substituted for an existing obligation," that definition would not exclude treating "rolled over" derivatives as constituting new value, as long as the "rollover" occurs upon the maturing of one derivative. That is to say, if derivative 1, with $20,000 of collateral securing a $15,000 obligation matures, is paid off (which involves no preference, as the counterparty is fully secured) and is replaced by derivative 2, with $40,000 of collateral securing a $15,000 obligation, there is no preference issue, even if the collateral (in both cases) declines by 50 percent by the time a bankruptcy case is commenced. Thus, even if a predictable response to subjecting derivatives to preference law would be to shorten the maturity of derivatives and rely on "rollover" derivatives, there is a world of difference between "opting out" of bankruptcy concerns with an *existing* transaction, and a series of shorter but independent transactions that run their ordinary course.

The preference concerns of a counterparty thus would focus on two other issues: **(a)** payment on the derivative within 90 days of bankruptcy when the payment exceeded the value of the collateral (that is, the counterparty was undersecured) and **(b)** transfers of new collateral to the counterparty within the 90-day preference period that increase (rather than through market forces) the value of the aggregate collateral securing the obligation to the counterparty. While **(a)** is a straight-out preference, **(b)** is more complicated.

To delve into that complication, it is useful to return to the analogy of the "two-point net improvement test" for cases where the collateral is inventory or receivables. The original idea behind the "two-point net improvement test" for inventory or receivables follows the image of a "pool" of collateral. One takes (for example) a security interest in "inventory," and knows that the inventory will fluctuate in value, not because of a change of market valuation of each individual item in that inventory, but because the nature of inventory is that it fluctuates in size. Thus, in the completely ordinary course of business, a security interest in an inventory of widgets, with each widget always worth $10, may fluctuate because the number of widgets in the inventory might be 8,000 on one day, 12,000 a week later, and 10,000 the following week. Viewing that this is unlikely to be the result of opt-out activity,[15] the Bankruptcy Code provides a safe harbor for such fluctuations, except to the extent that the creditor's overall position is better at the time of the commencement of the bankruptcy case than it was at a point 90 days earlier (or when credit was first extended within that 90-day period), § 547(c)(5). Thus, if the debtor owes $100,000 to the lender and the "pool" of widget inventory was worth $80,000 90 days before bankruptcy, declined to $60,000 30 days before bankruptcy, and then increased so that it was valued at $90,000 on the date of bankruptcy—all because of fluctuations in the number of widgets in the inventory—the creditor would have a potential voidable preference of $10,000, rather than $30,000.[16]

Derivatives are rarely secured by inventory or receivables, and therefore are not able to claim the protection of § 547(c)(5). But certain features of certain derivatives fit the underlying principle, in addition to being protected by the more general principle that changes in market values of underlying collateral are not themselves preferential, as discussed earlier.[17] For example, if a certain derivative transaction is secured by "all" of the debtor's mortgage-backed securities, and the quantity of those securities fluctuates, the

---

15. Which is not to say that it could not be, as where a creditor demands that its debtor "build up" its inventory within 90 days before bankruptcy.

16. The creditor may not even have a voidable preference in the amount of $10,000, as the trustee must also show that reduction in the creditor's unsecured claim was "to the prejudice of other creditors holding unsecured claims," § 547(c)(5), which may be difficult to show if all the debtor's other assets are worth exactly as much as before.

17. This would also protect the substitution of a new security as collateral when an old security matured, as long as the new security was not more valuable than the old.

analogy to inventory or receivables (which are protected by § 547(c)(2)) is strong and is deserving of comparable protection, which requires an amendment to § 547(c)(5) to include classes of securities or other "pool-like" collateral that might be the subject of derivative transactions in a Chapter 14 proceeding.

SUMMARY OF PROPOSED REVISIONS

I. Creation of a New Chapter 14

- Add a definition of a financial institution to § 101 to pick up institutions (including their subsidiaries) with assets more than $100 billion that are substantially engaged in providing financial services or financial products.
- Create a new Chapter 14 for financial institutions and require that financial institutions use it.
- Amend § 109 to provide that a financial institution must concurrently file for a Chapter 7 liquidation or a Chapter 11 reorganization at the time that it files for Chapter 14, and that all resulting proceedings will be conducted pursuant to Chapter 14.
- Create designated district court judges in the Second and DC Circuits to hear Chapter 14 cases, by adding a new provision to Title 28. Provide that these designated district court judges have exclusive jurisdiction over Chapter 14 cases notwithstanding the provisions of 28 U.S.C. § 157, and prohibit them from delegating the case to bankruptcy judges, but permitting them to assign to a special master, from a designated panel of special masters, the case and its proceedings as if it were a

designation to a bankruptcy judge under 28 U.S.C. § 158. Provide for the ability of the district judge to hire additional experts, as well as rely on the assistance of bankruptcy judges (subject to the prohibition on delegation of cases to such judges).

II. Commencing a Chapter 14 Case

- Revise § 109 to eliminate the exclusion from bankruptcy of insurance companies when Chapter 14 applies.
- Revise § 109 to eliminate the exclusion of stockbrokers and commodity brokers from Chapter 11 when Chapter 14 applies.
- Provide that the special subchapters in Chapter 7 for stockbrokers (§§ 741 et seq.) and commodity brokers (§§ 761 et seq.) do not apply when Chapter 14 applies.
- Adopt existing rules for the treatment of customer accounts currently in §§ 763 and 766 to apply to proceedings (whether liquidations or reorganizations) under Chapter 14.
- Provide that the SIPC (for stockbrokers) and the CFTC (for commodity brokers) have a right to be parties in relevant Chapter 14 cases.
- Amend § 303(b) and (h) to provide that the primary regulator may commence an involuntary case against a financial institution.
- Amend § 303(h) to permit an involuntary case commenced by the primary regulator to go forward if the financial institution's assets are less than its liabilities, at fair valuation, or the financial institution has unreasonably small capital.

III. Role of the Primary Regulator in Chapter 14; DIP Funding

- Provide that the regulators of the business of a covered financial institution or any subsidiary thereof would have standing with respect to the financial institution or the particular subsidiary to be heard or to raise motions relevant to their regulation with the Chapter 14 court.

- Amend § 363 to provide that the primary regulator has the power to file motions for the use, sale, or lease of property.

- Amend § 1121 to provide that, in a Chapter 14 case, notwithstanding § 1121(c), the primary regulator or a creditors' committee can file a plan of reorganization at any time after the order for relief.

- Amend § 364(b), (c), and (d) to make clear that, in a Chapter 14 case, DIP financing is permitted, upon court approval after motion and hearing instigated by the debtor-in-possession, the trustee, or the primary regulator, for the purpose of providing partial or complete payouts to some or all creditors, with petitioners for such funding bearing the burden of proof on **(a)** the necessity (for liquidity or other systemic reasons) of such payout (including its amount and the identified parties), **(b)** that such payout is less than or equal to a conservative estimate of the amount the creditors would receive in the bankruptcy proceeding without such funding, **(c)** that any such prepayments were not likely to favor particular creditors or otherwise undermine the operation of bankruptcy's priority rules, and **(d)** it shall be a provision of any such funding that, should the payout exceed the amount that the creditors would have received in the bankruptcy proceeding in the absence of such funding, either the creditors receiving such advanced payout agree to repay to the estate the amount by which their advanced payout exceeded that amount or the funder agrees to subordinate his claim to that of the other creditors to the extent necessary to allow them to receive what they would have received in bankruptcy in the absence of such funding. In addition, if the government is the source of the funds to make these prepayments, the petitioners for such funding will additionally be required to show that such funds are not available from a private party on reasonably equivalent terms.

IV. Qualified Financial Contracts in Chapter 14

- Automatic stay and repos: Amend § 362 to give the counterparty, in Chapter 14, the right to sell cash or cashlike collateral in its possession at any time, as well as the right to sell, upon petition, other financial (non–firm-specific) collateral in its possession upon a determination of the reasonable value of such collateral.
- Automatic stay and repos: Amend § 362 to give, in Chapter 14, a right of relief from the automatic stay upon petition by a counterparty seeking to sell collateral in the possession of the debtor to the extent the collateral consists of highly marketable securities or other cashlike collateral as well as, to the extent the collateral consists of other non–firm-specific collateral, upon the court's determination of its fair market value.
- Automatic stay and swaps: Limit the applicability of § 560 (as well as §§ 555 and 556) in Chapter 14 cases to the expiration of three days from the filing of a bankruptcy petition. After the expiration of that period, the counterparty has the right

to sell collateral in parallel to the provisions for collateral sales by repo counterparties in Chapter 14.

- Automatic stay and swaps: Clarify § 362(b)(17) so that a counterparty cannot offset, net out, or sell collateral until the debtor rejects the contract or the time period specified in § 560 expires.

- Automatic stay and repos/swaps: Make explicit that cross-termination and cross-collateralization provisions in master agreements remain effective notwithstanding termination—but not from repos to swaps (or vice versa) until both have been terminated.

- Trustee's avoiding powers, repos, and swaps: Provide that the provisions of § 546(f), (g), and (j) do not apply in a Chapter 14 proceeding.

- Trustee's avoiding powers, repos, and swaps: Amend § 547(c) (5) so that its "two-point net improvement" test applies to swaps in a Chapter 14 proceeding when the collateral can be identified as a defined "pool."

LEHMAN AND "ORDERLY LIQUIDATION"

3

Comment on Orderly Liquidation under Title II of Dodd-Frank and Chapter 14

WILLIAM F. KROENER III

There continues to be substantial debate whether Title II of Dodd-Frank, providing in limited circumstances for possible liquidation by the Federal Deposit Insurance Corporation (FDIC) of systemically important financial institutions (SIFIs), effectively eliminates "too big to fail." The FDIC staff has stated that it is open to proposed changes in law to allow more effective use of bankruptcy by financial intermediaries in order to minimize the need for use of Title II liquidations.[1] Chapter 14 of the bankruptcy law, developed as part of the Resolution Project and set forth in a separate chapter, is such a proposed change. Chapter 14 is intended to create a viable bankruptcy alternative that would be more consistent with bankruptcy practice than Title II "orderly liquidation." Chapter 14 would allow possible continued management participation and more extensive creditor involvement, and would eliminate substantial (and, in material respects, essentially unchallengeable) discretion that the FDIC has under Title II to effectively pick winners and losers among creditors in conducting a liquidation.

In that connection, the hypothetical example of the liquidation of Lehman under Title II, as set out in the FDIC's counterfactual

---

1. R. Christian Bruce, *Krimminger's List: A Little More Chapter 11, A Little Less Title II*, Banking Daily (BNA), Dec. 13, 2011.

presentation of how the FDIC would have conducted the orderly liquidation of Lehman under the Dodd-Frank Act,[2] suggests a number of difficulties in the existing bankruptcy laws that are addressed and largely eliminated by the proposed Chapter 14. The FDIC counterfactual on orderly liquidation of Lehman concludes that liquidation of Lehman under Title II of Dodd-Frank would have resulted in a recovery rate for unsecured creditors of 97 cents on the dollar,[3] significantly more than creditors are expected to receive in the Lehman bankruptcy. As discussed in section II of this chapter, however, this conclusion likely overstates potential recoveries. Orderly liquidation of Lehman by the FDIC under Title II likely would have involved a wide range of possible more negative outcomes. The thesis of this chapter is that reorganization or liquidation of Lehman under the proposed Chapter 14—as compared to liquidation by the FDIC under Title II, under consistent assumptions (either the FDIC's or more neutral ones)—could produce preferable results and more knowledgeable valuations in most situations without implicating "too big to fail" concerns and while better protecting all creditors. A further purpose is to identify numerous overoptimistic assumptions in the FDIC's Lehman counterfactual to facilitate a more nuanced comparison with an alternative Chapter 14 resolution.

At the outset, it should be noted that in effecting "orderly liquidations" the FDIC is likely to use its discretion in a manner similar to its practices under the Federal Deposit Insurance Act (FDIA) to avoid real liquidation of business operations. The possibility of "conservatorship" as such was prohibited by the Boxer Amendment as part of the legislative process.[4] However, the FDIC can (and has

---

2. *The Orderly Liquidation of Lehman Brothers Holdings Inc. under the Dodd-Frank Act*, 5(2) FDIC Quarterly 31–49 (2011).

3. *Id.* at 48.

4. Dodd-Frank Act, Pub. L. 111–203 (July 21, 2010), § 214.

admitted that it will) reach effectively the same result in another way. The FDIC has indicated that it will allow continuing operation by new management of the business in a "bridge" financial institution in order to maximize value when an immediate sale in a purchase and assumption transaction to a third party is not available. It can be seriously disputed whether this is a true "liquidation." In any event, however, as recognized by the trend of modern bankruptcy law and contemplated as possible in Chapter 14, continued operation—especially by knowledgeable existing management—may produce better valuations and more successful operations.

I. TITLE II, THE FDIA, AND CHAPTER 14

The FDIC has argued that its discretion is substantially limited in liquidations under Title II and that "too big to fail" has been eliminated with respect to nonbank financial intermediaries.[5] Close examination suggests that (1) in the actual exercise of its liquidation authority, the FDIC has essentially the same wide discretion historically exercised in the case of failed banks under the FDIA, notably in determining those assets and liabilities to transfer to a bridge institution; and (2) the FDIC's use of bridge financial institutions, in an effort to substantially preserve going concern value, is likely to be a principal approach under Title II and may effectively allow continuation rather than liquidation of the business of the failed company, notwithstanding claims to the contrary by Congress

---

5. Sheila C. Bair, "We Must Resolve to End Too Big to Fail," Remarks before the 47th Annual Conference on Bank Structure and Competition, sponsored by the Federal Reserve Bank of Chicago, May 5, 2011, reprinted in 5(2) FDIC Quarterly 25–29 (2011).

and the FDIC.[6] Moreover, the FDIC's discretion is likely to be exercised in a manner adverse (perhaps necessarily so) to the interests of some disfavored creditors.[7] The successful operation of Orderly Liquidation Authority (OLA) under Title II depends on the exercise by the FDIC of its substantial discretion so as to avoid a central feature of Title II: liquidation, as opposed to continuation of the business in another form. This could be regarded as the continuation of past "too big to fail" policies and the accompanying moral hazard, just in a modified form. By comparison, Chapter 14 affords a method both for realizing greater value by continuing knowledgeable management in place and for allowing a distribution of that value to creditors in a manner more consistent with U.S. bankruptcy law and expectations and more equally among creditors of the same class.

There are, of course, some differences between the FDIC's discretion in the operation of liquidation authority under Title II of Dodd-Frank and in bank resolutions under the FDIA. These, however, do not change the overall fact: the FDIC has very substantial discretion, in important respects unconstrained by judicial oversight, under Title II. Among the differences between Dodd-Frank and the FDIC operations under the FDIA, the most notable that might be cited are: (1) the broader decision-making process involving the Federal Reserve, the U.S. Treasury, and the president to invoke orderly liquidation, similar to the process for systemic (but not most) bank failures under the FDIA; (2) the (nominal) requirement that the covered financial institution be liquidated; (3) the purported limited time period for completion of the liquidation; (4) certain differences in creditor priorities; and (5) involvement in appropriate instances

---

6. Dodd-Frank, § 204(a); *Orderly Liquidation of Lehman Brothers Holdings Inc.* (*supra* n. 2), 36.
7. Kenneth E. Scott, *A Guide to the Resolution of Failed Financial Institutions: Dodd-Frank Title II and Proposed Chapter 14*, chapter 1 in this volume.

of other functional regulators—the Securities and Exchange Commission (SEC), Securities Investor Protection Corporation (SIPC), and state insurance regulators. In fact, once a liquidation under Title II is determined to be invoked, these differences have little effect on FDIC practice. While it is true that other entities have a role in the initial decision to liquidate a covered financial company under Title II, it is the FDIC that formulates and carries out the resolution.

Under the FDIA, the FDIC has used "bridge" banks generally only in situations where no bidder has come forward due to fraud, a rapid failure for liquidity reasons, or other reasons of wide uncertainty as to values. Such situations may be expected to occur more frequently in the case of the possible failure of systemically important financial companies in the variations listed by Kenneth Scott—macro shocks, chain reactions, and common abrupt reassessments.[8] There is general agreement that such events could trigger liquidity runs and sudden changes. In such cases (and notably contrary to the Lehman counterfactual set out by the FDIC staff), it is not possible for the FDIC to have done extensive investigation and valuation and conducted an auction bidding procedure. So to preserve value, as noted previously, the FDIC would not "liquidate" the business in any commonly understood meaning of the term, but would use a "bridge" financial institution as an interim step and transfer substantial amounts of assets and liabilities to the bridge institution, thereby picking winners and losers among the creditors and effectively continuing the business.

Because of the likely rapidity of the failure of these institutions, the FDIC is unlikely to be able to use the extensive investigation and valuation procedures relied upon in the FDIC Lehman counterfactual. Instead, the FDIC is likely to use bridge institutions

---

8. *Id.* at 14–16.

much more frequently under Title II than it has under the FDIA. Even where there is sufficient time to plan for orderly liquidation, as assumed by the FDIC in its Lehman counterfactual, the FDIC would be transferring some assets and favored liabilities to a purchaser (rather than a bridge institution) while disfavoring others. The FDIC's practice in transferring assets and liabilities to bridge banks has varied, but generally has encompassed those items it views necessary or essential for continued operations, leaving behind claims as of the date of failure and assets where there may be questions of value. The FDIC has made an effort to assure maximum equal treatment in orderly liquidations in its new rule in 12 C.F.R. § 380.27(4), but that is a procedural protection (requiring FDIC Board action rather than FDIC staff decisions) that does not limit FDIC discretion in any substantive manner. By comparison, in the framework of the new Chapter 14, knowledgeable management could be allowed to remain in place and could itself accomplish the same value preservation; creditors would be afforded traditional rights of legal recourse and equal treatment. Moreover, by narrowing the circumstances where orderly liquidation might be necessary, Chapter 14 would eliminate some of the uncertainties as to outcomes and thereby reduce costs.

II. THE LEHMAN CASE

This brings us to consideration of some of the specifics of the FDIC's Lehman counterfactual on "orderly liquidation" under Title II. The FDIC's analysis raises a number of questions. First and most important, there is an assumption of complete, up-to-date information possessed by the FDIC and other regulators. In order to derive its claimed recovery, facts are cited from the record of later court proceedings and the examiner's report. These facts are assumed to be known *ex ante* by virtue of the examination authority and on-site supervision by the FDIC. This state of knowledge is unrealistic in the real world in the case of a rapid liquidity failure of a large financial institution in one or more of the scenarios previously identified. Extensive past experience indicates that information regarding failing institutions can be very far from robust, and failures can arise very suddenly. The most recent example, which hopefully will not often be repeated, is the failure of MF Global, where for almost six months approximately $1.6 billion in assets remained missing; although those assets apparently have now been located, it remains unclear whether any are recoverable.[9] This uncertainty and lack of full information arises often in the failure of smaller banks and invariably in larger failures. Consider, for example, the case of Wachovia, where the FDIC had initially agreed to a less-favorable bid from Citigroup that would have cost considerably more than the ultimate acquisition by Wells Fargo.

Second, the FDIC Lehman counterfactual assumes complete and largely transparent coordination with foreign regulators and the absence of international complications or adverse foreign court rulings that would impede the liquidation by the FDIC. As shown in Kimberly Summe's presentation and noted elsewhere,[10] this is contrary to what actually happened in Lehman, where substantial funds were trapped offshore in foreign subsidiaries. The FDIC has admitted that developing a better understanding of the international aspects

---

9. Testimony of James W. Giddens, Trustee for the Securities Investor Protection Act Liquidation of MF Global Inc. before the U.S. Senate Committee on Banking, Housing and Urban Affairs, April 24, 2012.

10. Kimberly Anne Summe, *An Examination of Lehman Brothers' Derivatives Portfolio Postbankruptcy: Would Dodd-Frank Have Made a Difference?* chapter 4 in this volume.

of orderly liquidation and better knowledge of and relationships with foreign financial regulators is a subject that needs far more attention and progress. The FDIC staff has also noted that there is little likelihood there could be an international treaty on financial institution resolution. In fact, the Lehman bankruptcy entailed numerous international complications and the need ultimately for a formal protocol among creditors. It is unrealistic in the face of this past experience and the current state of international cooperation to believe that the orderly liquidation of Lehman could have been effected speedily without material international complications.

Third, and related to the second point, the counterfactual focuses only on the top company, Lehman Brothers Holdings Inc., and ignores the possible effects of related liquidation, bankruptcy, or other proceedings in the United States or abroad involving subsidiaries and affiliates of Lehman. There is also material risk that U.S. domestic subsidiaries and operations will be distressed and may need reorganization or resolution, further complicating matters. In fact, there were a number of significant proceedings in Lehman involving subsidiaries and affiliates and intercompany obligations,[11] and ultimately it was necessary to agree on an extensive cross-border insolvency protocol among creditors. Among the international issues arising in the Lehman proceedings were allegations of automatic stay violations, conflicting U.S.-U.K. judgments, cross-border valuation questions, intercompany claims, subordination conflicts, and others.[12] The concept that the top Lehman company could be

---

11. *See*, for example, Lehman International Proceedings, in the International Protocol Proposal, Presentation to the Bankruptcy Court by Alvarez & Marsal (Feb. 11, 2009); Presentation to the American Bar Association, Business Law Section, Spring Meeting (April 15, 2011); and ABA Business Law Section, Annual Meeting Materials (August 2011).

12. Milbank, Tweed, Hadley, & McCloy, "Lehman Failure Replayed: Would FDIC Liquidation Be More Orderly than Bankruptcy?" Presentation to the Ameri-

liquidated under Title II without complications from subsidiaries and affiliates is not warranted. And some of these complications could occur in a purely domestic context as well.

Fourth, the FDIC assumption about funding in its Lehman counterfactual may also be unrealistic. The FDIC simply asserts that sufficient funding would be available because there is no need for court approval. However, § 210(n)(6)(A) of Dodd-Frank explicitly limits available funding for the FDIC to 10 percent of the book value of the consolidated assets for the first 30 days or until there has been a valuation of the assets of the covered financial company. It appears that an amount in excess of this 10 percent book value would have been needed immediately to cover collateral obligations and meet Lehman's debt problems.[13] At a minimum, this could result in the necessity for either a very rushed and suspect valuation of assets and positions or a very quick need for third-party financing guaranteed by the FDIC to avoid that restriction.

Fifth, the FDIC's counterfactual identifies resolution plans (the so-called "living wills") that might have been prepared by Lehman as giving orderly liquidation under Title II an advantage over bankruptcy proceedings. Of course, this advantage should be at least equally available under Chapter 14. In fact, under § 165 of Dodd-Frank, these resolution plans are required to be prepared for resolution of the covered financial company under the bankruptcy law rather than under Title II. Thus, insofar as detailed advance planning had been in fact accomplished by Lehman (or in the future by

---

can Bar Association, Business Law Section, Spring Meeting (April 15, 2011); ABA Business Law Section, Annual Meeting Materials (August 2011).

13. The FDIC staff has indicated that, in any event, this limitation may be avoided by the FDIC guaranteeing third-party indebtedness to fund the bridge institution, since guarantees are valued based on the risk of payment rather than their face value.

other entities), it would seem more useful in a bankruptcy proceeding (under Chapter 14, if it were put in place) than in a Title II FDIC liquidation. An additional advantage, previously noted, would be that a Chapter 14 bankruptcy proceeding could be initiated and possibly overseen by continuing management that prepared the living will and has full current knowledge of the operations.

Sixth, the FDIC counterfactual notes the advantage of the ability of the FDIC to briefly delay, close out, and possibly transfer to third parties qualified financial contracts under Title II. Assuming these are important steps, despite the doubts raised by Summe's analysis,[14] these advantages would be similarly available under the proposed Chapter 14 since the governing provisions are similar, albeit more narrowly tailored to firm-specific collateral.

Seventh, as noted elsewhere,[15] the FDIC counterfactual makes unrealistic assumptions as to value in concluding that unsecured creditors would have achieved a 97 percent return on claims. Specifically, the FDIC assumes that only the "suspect" assets (of from $50 billion to $70 billion) would lose any value and all other asset values would remain stable for the orderly liquidation. This seems very unrealistic in any situation of serious distress.

Eighth, and significantly, in assessing the likely recovery by unsecured creditors in its counterfactual, the FDIC explicitly assumes that "losses had been distributed equally among all of Lehman's remaining unsecured creditors." This is, of course, substantially what would happen under Chapter 14, but contrary to how the FDIC might distribute losses in liquidation under Title II (unless "remaining" is read to exclude unsecured creditors whose claims are trans-

14. Summe, *An Examination of Lehman Brothers' Derivatives Portfolio Postbankruptcy* (*supra* n. 10), pp. 85–129.

15. Stephen J. Lubben, *The F.D.I.C.'s Lehman Fantasy*, New York Times, Dealbook Column (April 19, 2011).

ferred to the bridge institution; in which case, the meaning of "equally" is distorted). In a liquidation under Title II, the FDIC has substantial discretion (similar to that the FDIC exercises in resolutions of insured banks) in determining whether to transfer claims to a bridge institution or leave them behind in the receivership. Claims that are transferred to the bridge institution, if it operates in accordance with FDIC expectations,[16] end up fully paid with any excess amounts returned to the receivership. Claimants remaining behind in the receivership, by contrast, are entitled only to claim *pro rata* by claim priority what is ultimately available from the receivership assets, which for general, unsecured creditors is almost always considerably less than a full 100 cents on the dollar. The FDIC in its counterfactual neither details the differences among creditors as to winners or losers, nor explains how the latter would be assured a minimum recovery of what they might have received in an actual bankruptcy liquidation.

Finally, the FDIC counterfactual assumes a successful sale of business to a third party, something that would be equally possible under Chapter 14. The bidding under Chapter 14 would be competitive and subject to judicial overdraft and scrutiny.

III. CONCLUSION

The FDIC's counterfactual is, in sum, a comparison of the actual unplanned liquidation of Lehman under current bankruptcy law with retrospective application of Title II using assumptions of perfect

---

16. It is possible, of course, that these expectations could be overoptimistic and the bridge institution could in turn fail or have to be liquidated with creditors receiving less than their full claimed amount.

knowledge and value stability. In a Title II liquidation, there is no possibility of continuing prior "responsible" management, no creditors' committee, no court monitoring, and the absence of equal treatment of similarly situated creditors. The FDIC unilaterally makes all the decisions, and these are final in all respects. By contrast, Chapter 14 restores these features of traditional bankruptcy, provides greater clarity of application, and is intended to avoid some of the key problems that have been troublesome in the Lehman proceedings.

For all of these reasons, the FDIC's Lehman counterfactual is subject to considerable doubt. In some cases, the operating assumptions are too optimistic; the problems of imperfect knowledge and the difficulties of international coordination are ignored; and the claimed advantages over bankruptcy result from aspects of existing bankruptcy law that would be substantially addressed by the proposed Chapter 14. Therefore, a full counterfactual Lehman bankruptcy comparing a Title II liquidation with Chapter 14 on a common baseline, with realistic assumptions as to the state of knowledge and international complications, would be a more effective way to test the asserted superiority of Title II.

4

An Examination of Lehman Brothers' Derivatives Portfolio Postbankruptcy

Would Dodd-Frank Have Made a Difference?

Kimberly Anne Summe

I. INTRODUCTION

In the three and a half years since 157-year-old Lehman Brothers made the largest bankruptcy filing in U.S. history, the regulatory and financial landscape has shifted in many ways. As expected after any market crash of such severity and duration, policy makers considered, among many issues, whether the U.S. Bankruptcy Code had functioned effectively, and concluded that it had not. Ben S. Bernanke, chairman of the Board of Governors of the Federal Reserve System, testified to the House Committee on Financial Services on October 1, 2009, that:

> In most cases, the federal bankruptcy laws provide an appropriate framework for the resolution of nonbank financial institutions. However, the bankruptcy code does not sufficiently protect the public's strong interest in ensuring the orderly resolution of a nonbank financial firm whose failure would pose substantial risks to the financial system and to the economy. Indeed, after Lehman Brothers' and AIG's experiences, there is little doubt that we need a third

option between the choices of bankruptcy and bailout for such firms.[1]

Congress and the White House enshrined that third option into Title II of the Wall Street Reform and Consumer Protection Act ("Dodd-Frank"), signed into law by President Obama on July 21, 2010. Title II of Dodd-Frank promulgated an entirely new insolvency regime for large, interconnected financial companies whose possible failure would portend the sort of economic devastation that policy makers assumed the Lehman Brothers bankruptcy unleashed.

The purpose of this chapter is to examine how Lehman Brothers' bankruptcy has unfolded to date with respect to its U.S. derivatives portfolio and how that would be different had Dodd-Frank been in effect in September 2008.[2] It concludes that, with respect to the derivatives portfolio of any failed company captured by the resolution procedures of Title II of Dodd-Frank, Congress's efforts neither resulted in a significant change to the way derivative trades are handled postbankruptcy nor provided comfort that a government bailout of the clearinghouses that are an important feature of the new regime will be avoided.

II. LEHMAN BROTHERS—HOW HAS ITS DERIVATIVES PORTFOLIO FARED POSTBANKRUPTCY?

Contemporary financial institutions, particularly those that are arguably most systemically important, operate globally. A mix of

---

1. Testimony of Ben S. Bernanke, Chairman of the Board of Governors of the Federal Reserve System, to the U.S. House of Representatives Committee on Financial Services (October 1, 2009), 7.

2. This chapter is based on publicly available information through February 3, 2012.

banks, broker-dealers, commodity brokers, futures commission merchants, and corporations and insurance companies under the financial institution's umbrella engage in business twenty-four hours a day, seven days a week, in dozens of jurisdictions. Upon insolvency, each entity becomes subject to its own insolvency regime, dependent upon its jurisdictional location, its organizational form, and its activities. Lehman Brothers' bankruptcy, in the broadest sense, involved five bodies of laws applicable to its various corporate entities: (1) the Federal Deposit Insurance Act applied to its U.S. banks;[3] (2) the Bankruptcy Code applied to its insolvent corporations, such as its Delaware corporations that traded derivatives, including Lehman Brothers Special Financing, Inc.; (3) the Securities Investor Protection Act regime applied to the insolvent broker-dealer, Lehman Brothers Inc.; (4) state insurance laws applied to its insurance subsidiaries; and (5) more than 80 jurisdictions' insolvency laws applied to the insolvent non-U.S. Lehman Brothers entities.[4]

Lehman Brothers Special Financing, Inc. (LBSF) was the primary, although not the exclusive, entity through which Lehman Brothers' U.S. derivatives business was done. Outside of the United States, derivatives transactions were done through Lehman Brothers

---

3. The federal bankruptcy court in Manhattan approved the sale of Aurora Bank FSB, formerly known as Lehman Brothers Bank, and ordered the sale to be complete by May 2012. Woodlands Commercial Bank, formerly known as Lehman Brothers Commercial Bank, went out of business on December 30, 2011.

4. Lehman Brothers Holdings Inc.—The State of the Estate, http://www.srz .com/files/upload/Alerts/Lehman_Brothers_State_of_the_Estate.pdf (September 22, 2010), 8. *See also* Financial Crisis Inquiry Commission, *The Final Report of the National Commission of the Causes of the Financial and Economic Crisis in the United States*, http://fcic.law.stanford.edu/report (January 2011), 340. Note that, as discussed in this volume, the Resolution Project has recommended a new addition to the U.S. Bankruptcy Code, Chapter 14, which would reduce the number of bankruptcy proceedings for systemically important entities and would capture previously distinct provisions applicable to stockbrokers, commodity brokers, and domestic and foreign insurance companies.

International (Europe) (LBIE).[5] When Lehman Brothers filed for bankruptcy, the U.S. estate reported that it was a counterparty to 930,000 derivatives transactions documented under 6,120 International Swaps and Derivatives Association (ISDA) Master Agreements.[6] The vast majority of those derivatives transactions involved LBSF, a Delaware corporation, with documentation being executed pursuant to the industry standard ISDA Master Agreement.[7] While the exact size of LBSF's derivatives portfolio in September 2008, on a prebankruptcy basis, has not been published, Lehman Brothers' global derivatives portfolio was estimated to be $35 trillion in notional value, representing about 5 percent of derivatives transactions globally.[8] In addition, the Examiner's Report to the U.S. Bankruptcy Court noted that the Lehman Brothers' U.S. derivatives portfolio had a net value of $21 billion as of May 31, 2008.[9] That net value equaled 3.3 percent of Lehman Brothers' total assets.[10]

Under the ISDA Master Agreement, upon a counterparty's (or guarantor's) default, such as a voluntary or involuntary bankruptcy, the nondefaulting party has the right to designate a date on which the portfolio of derivatives will be valued and terminated, to terminate the transactions on such date, and to liquidate and apply any

---

5. Note that this chapter does not address how derivatives claims against LBIE are proceeding.

6. Lehman Brothers Holdings Inc. First Creditors Section 341 Meeting, http://dm .epiq11.com/lehman/Document (January 29, 2009), 19–20. Note that Lehman Brothers Holdings Inc.—The State of the Estate, http://dm.epiq11.com/lehman/Document (November 18, 2009), 28, reports a slightly different figure of 6,355 contracts.

7. Other U.S. Lehman entities engaged in derivatives trading, but LBSF was by far the largest among the U.S. entities trading.

8. Bank for International Settlements, *Semiannual Over-the-Counter (OTC) Derivatives Markets Statistics*, www.bis.org/statistics (June 2009).

9. Report of Anton R. Valukas, Examiner, to the U.S. Bankruptcy Court, http:// lehmanreport.jenner.com (March 11, 2010), 569.

10. *Id.*

collateral. Once Lehman Brothers Holdings Inc. filed for bankruptcy on September 15, 2008, its status as the guarantor for LBSF's derivatives transactions meant that nondefaulting parties were able to elect to terminate their transactions, even though LBSF did not file for bankruptcy until October 3, 2008. Approximately 80 percent of the derivatives counterparties to LBSF terminated their derivatives transactions under the ISDA Master Agreement within five weeks of bankruptcy.[11]

The estate was successful in capturing receivables almost immediately postbankruptcy. On September 14, 2008, the estate reported that LBSF had a then-current cash position of $7 million. Within three and a half months, LBSF had a current cash position of $925 million.[12] By November 18, 2009, the Lehman estate reported that figure had grown dramatically to $5.025 billion in current cash and investments for LBSF;[13] adding in the other U.S. entities involved in trading derivatives increased that figure to $8 billion.[14] By June 30, 2010, LBSF had approximately $7.355 billion in current cash and investments,[15] and $11.467 billion when other U.S. Lehman entities were included.[16] By February 1, 2011, LBSF had $8.79 billion in current cash and investments,[17] and $15 billion in aggregate being

11. Debtors' Motion for an Order pursuant to Sections 105 and 365 of the Bankruptcy Code to Establish Procedures for the Settlement or Assumption and Assignment of Prepetition Derivatives Contracts, Lehman Brothers Holdings Inc., et al., No. 08-13555 (U.S. Bankr. Ct. S.D.N.Y., November 13, 2008).

12. Lehman Brothers Holdings Inc. First Creditors Section 341 Meeting (*supra* n. 6), 6 (reflects figures as of January 2, 2009).

13. Lehman Brothers Holdings Inc.—The State of the Estate (November 18, 2009), 9.

14. *Id.* at 26.

15. Lehman Brothers Holdings Inc.—The State of the Estate (September 22, 2010), 10.

16. *Id.* at 11.

17. Lehman Brothers Holdings Inc., Monthly Operating Report, http://idc.api.edgar-online.com (March 18, 2011).

received to the credit of the estate.[18] LBSF represents nearly half of all cash and cash investment positions in the Lehman Brothers estate as compared to the aggregate of all Lehman U.S. debtor entities.[19]

While the administrator has worked effectively to increase the assets of the estate, as noted previously, and the ISDA Master Agreement offered a well-understood process and approach to calculating the value of terminated transactions, these factors have not lessened the sheer magnitude of effort involved in the most complex derivatives business unwinding in history. While the vast majority of counterparties quickly terminated their derivatives transactions with U.S. Lehman Brothers entities, including LBSF, that termination under the contractual mechanics did not mean the process was at an end. Rather, a multistep process was required for reconciling, reviewing counterparty valuations of the terminated transactions, and then moving to settlement. The last time Lehman Brothers published its resolution process figures in November 2009, 61 percent of derivatives claims had been reconciled and 50 percent had their valuation completed.[20] In that same report, the estate reported that LBSF had 3,222 claims against it, presumably all or mostly all derivatives claims since that was LBSF's principal business. At the time, this figure represented 5 percent by volume and 11 percent by dollars of the top five debtor entities' claims in aggregate.[21]

---

18. Lehman Brothers Holdings Inc., Plan Status Report, http://www.dm.epiq11.com/lehman/Document (January 13, 2011), 16.

19. Lehman Brothers Holdings Inc.—The State of the Estate (September 22, 2010), 10.

20. Lehman Brothers Holdings Inc.—The State of the Estate (November 18, 2009), 28.

21. *Id.* at 32. Duplicate claims were often filed against LBSF and the parent company, but LBSF had a relatively small percentage of the claims made against the various U.S. Lehman Brothers entities, as most were understandably against the parent company.

As the estate's work progressed, the administrator took the view that many counterparties were inflating their derivatives claims. Daniel Ehrmann, a managing director at Alvarez & Marsal and co-head of derivatives at Lehman Brothers Holdings Inc., stated: "We discovered that out of all the claims against the Lehman estate, those in the derivatives subset were most inflated."[22] In fact, in April 2010, Lehman Brothers Holdings Inc. sued Nomura Holdings Inc., arguing that Nomura's $720 million of derivatives claims relating to 2,464 transactions were the product of "egregious inflation" and reflected a desire to "secure a windfall" from Lehman's bankruptcy at the expense of creditors.[23] Indeed, the week prior to Lehman Brothers' bankruptcy, Nomura reported that it owed more than $200 million to LBSF.[24] At the time of this writing, the case had not settled.

While the mechanics of the ISDA Master Agreement functioned effectively (and quickly postbankruptcy) so that the vast majority of derivatives transactions were terminated, the legal obligations imposed on the administrator are such that a high standard of care is required before claims can be finalized for settlement. The statutory duties of the trustee in a Chapter 11 case are set forth in § 1106 of the U.S. Bankruptcy Code.[25] In addition, case law imposes fiduciary obligations on a trustee, including treating all beneficiaries fairly and equally.[26] With thousands of derivatives claims, the administrator has a fiduciary duty to review and reconcile the process and conduct of how each nondefaulting party reached its early

---

22. Matt Cameron, "LBHI Administrators Push for Settlement of Derivatives Claims," *Risk*, March 2, 2011.

23. Adversary Complaint and Objection filed by Lehman Brothers Holdings Inc. in Bankr. Ct. S.D.N.Y. (April 23, 2010), 2.

24. *Id.* at 3.

25. 11 U.S.C. § 1106.

26. Restatement (Second) of Trusts, §§ 170, 174, and 183.

termination amount relating to each derivative trade—this for more than 6,000 counterparties and around one million transactions. The goal of this painstaking but required process is to ensure that no creditor is preferred over another and to maximize the size of the estate for the benefit of all creditors. Practically, what this means is that the administrator's staff conducts daily meetings with creditors to review the proposed settlement of each derivative claim—in essence, the early termination amount for each individual derivative transaction must be reviewed in accordance with the administrator's fiduciary duty requirements to ensure that the estate's beneficiaries are being treated fairly and equally.

The settlement of the derivatives portfolio should be considered in the context of the overall bankruptcy process to date. On March 15, 2010, Lehman Brothers Holdings Inc. and its 22 affiliated Chapter 11 debtors filed a joint Chapter 11 plan with the U.S. Bankruptcy Court for the Southern District of New York. The following month, Lehman Brothers filed its liquidation plan with the bankruptcy court. The liquidation plan called for maintaining the corporate distinction of each Lehman entity that had filed for bankruptcy in 2008. This approach ensured that each affiliate would make payments to its creditors on the basis of its own asset base. However, creditors of the parent company, Lehman Brothers Holdings Inc., argued that parent company guarantees of affiliates such as LBSF meant that more debt resided at the parent level while more assets were at the subsidiary level. For example, after the liquidation plan was filed in April 2010, Lehman Brothers Holdings Inc. reported $2 billion in cash and investments on June 30, 2010, whereas LBSF had $7.35 billion in cash and investments.[27] Perhaps not surprisingly,

---

27. Lehman Brothers Holdings Inc.—The State of the Estate (September 22, 2010), 10.

a group of 10 creditors led by Paulson & Co., Canyon Partners LLC, the California Public Employees Retirement System, and Pacific Investment Management Company countered with their own liquidation plan to consolidate all affiliates' assets into one Lehman entity—resulting in holders of parent company claims receiving more than if the corporate entity structure remained intact. This group of 10 represented $20 billion of Lehman Brothers Holdings Inc. claims, including $16 billion of senior bonds.[28] In essence, this group of bondholders wanted to reduce the assets available to the derivatives creditors to the benefit of the bondholders.

In response, on January 25, 2011, Lehman Brothers filed an amended version of its liquidation plan seeking compromise with those creditors.[29] The new plan retained the corporate formalities of each debtor entity, but redistributed the payouts made to certain creditors. In essence, between 20 and 30 percent of payments owed to creditors of various operating companies, such as LBSF, would be forfeited and reallocated to the parent company's creditors. For example, under Lehman Brothers' April 2010 liquidation plan, derivatives creditors of LBSF—such as Bank of America, Credit Suisse, and Goldman Sachs—would have received a 24.1 percent payout, while under the amended January 2011 liquidation plan, those derivatives creditors would have received a 22.3 percent payout while creditors of the parent entity received slightly more than originally proposed.

The differing views among Lehman Brothers' creditors rested on the disparity of the recovery pool available to counterparties of LBSF and the recovery pool available to bondholders and other creditors of the parent company. Jostling among these groups coincided with

---

28. Linda Sandler and David McLaughlin, "Lehman's $61 Billion Plan Has Carrot, Stick for Paulson-Calpers," *Bloomberg*, January 26, 2011.

29. *See* www.lehmancreditors.com for a copy of the liquidation plan.

the administrator's efforts to find a more streamlined mechanism to settle greater numbers of derivatives claims. According to the *Plan Status Report* submitted to the bankruptcy court on January 13, 2011, out of $45.4 billion in claims made with regard to derivatives transactions, only $5 billion (or 11 percent) had been settled by the Lehman administrator by January 2011.[30] As noted previously, there was frustration on the part of the administrator that, at best, there were duplicative derivatives claims submitted and, at worst, exaggerated derivatives claims. In an effort to address the fact that 48 percent of those outstanding claims, or $22 billion, were from 30 of Lehman Brothers' largest bank counterparties, the estate changed its tactics for resolution. Citing the time and costs involved in settling the remaining derivatives claims, Lehman Brothers asserted that it would develop "consistent, transparent, derivative valuation rules."[31] Following months of meetings with some of its largest bank counterparties, the estate published its Derivatives Claims Settlement Framework (the "framework") on May 31, 2011.[32]

The framework offered a standardized methodology for valuing the remaining derivatives claims. The estate proposed to establish the date and time for the calculation of midmarket values for the terminated transactions, calculate the midmarket values, and account for collateral and cash payments, among other items.[33] Specifying a uniform time for the calculation of values for terminated transactions may not seem like a big deal and, in fact, it may even appear to be fair as it applies equally to all parties bound by the framework, but it can lead to significant disparity in outcomes. For

---

30. Lehman Brothers Holdings Inc.—Plan Status Report (*supra* n. 18).

31. *Id.* at 17.

32. Lehman Brothers Holdings Inc., Derivatives Claims Settlement Framework, http://dm.epiq11.com/lehman/Document (May 31, 2011).

33. *Id.* at 5.

example, the framework proposed that the preponderance of a big bank's transactions that terminated on or prior to Friday, September 19, 2008, would be valued on one single business day during the week of September 15, 2008. That approach intentionally overlooked the fact that significant intraday fluctuations occurred on Monday, September 15, for example, the date that the parent company filed for bankruptcy. Moreover, it jettisoned the fact that different legal entities located in different geographic regions globally were the nondefaulting parties. For example, a nondefaulting party located in Japan would be forced to select the same termination date as a nondefaulting party located in New York, even though the former, under the governing contract for the transaction, would be permitted to terminate 13 hours earlier in an entirely different market. This approach, particularly in the volatile markets following the Lehman Brothers' bankruptcy filing, pushed efficiency ahead of contractual rights.

While details of the component transactions representing Lehman Brothers' derivatives portfolio are not public, based on data that the Office of the Comptroller of the Currency (OCC) and the Bank for International Settlements (BIS) publish, one could reasonably assume based on the last filing made by the estate on May 31, 2008, that the majority of its portfolio represented interest rate and foreign exchange derivatives.[34] If we assume that Lehman Brothers' derivatives portfolio was reasonably proximate to that of other large banks, the bulk of the outstanding transactions were interest rate swaps, the most ubiquitous derivative. Hence, the selection of one point in time for the valuation of that transaction type may be problematic. Interest

---

34. Report of Anton R. Valukas, Examiner, to the U.S. Bankruptcy Court, http://lehmanreport.jenner.com (March 10, 2011), 572. Note that, unfortunately, interest rates and credit default swaps are combined into one category in the May 31, 2008, filing.

rate swaps, for example, are not typically closed out at the same time on the same day, as trades may be booked in different jurisdictions and therefore time zones. For example, the BIS triennial survey reported that for all interest rate and foreign exchange derivatives, 70 percent of trading occurs with counterparties outside the United States.[35] This aspect of the market may make it more challenging for the administrator to argue that it is fair to select one point in time to value the terminated transactions.

In addition, the framework proposed to reduce the number of maturity "buckets" used for aggregating and offsetting exposures and to have Lehman Brothers determine the bid-ask spread that is typically provided by the nondefaulting party. To date, when a derivatives portfolio is being terminated, the components of that portfolio are divided into buckets organized by maturity of the individual transaction type. The nondefaulting party can then net those exposures. A bid-offer adjustment is often made to the netted exposure amount—a cost to the defaulting party and one that represents uncollateralized risk. The challenge in closing out transactions in the volatile markets of September and October 2008 meant that more bid-offers were included in the nondefaulting parties' closeout prices and fewer exposures were netted. The administrator's postcontract reduction of the number of maturity buckets meant that the bid-offer adjustment would be retroactively reduced, thereby significantly impacting the value of the terminated transactions. Thus, while spreads on normally liquid transactions, such as interest rate swaps, increased in the aftermath of Lehman Brothers' bankruptcy, the administrator imposed a narrower and more uniform

---

35. Federal Reserve Bank of New York, "The Foreign Exchange and Interest Rate Derivatives Markets: Turnover in the United States" (April 2010), 9–10. Note that this survey is coordinated by the BIS with 53 central banks in April of every third year.

approach that will minimize the valuations produced by those volatile markets.

The framework that Lehman Brothers proposed essentially concluded that the methodology for valuing terminated transactions under an ISDA Master Agreement should shift in an effort to address the formidable stack of derivatives claims. The administrator's goal of providing "consistent, transparent, derivative valuation rules" is certainly achieved through the framework: the methodology is published and therefore transparent. In addition, adherents to the framework will experience significant cost savings of time and resources.

Ultimately, virtually all creditors agreed to support the framework and its inclusion in the Third Amended Joint Chapter 11 Plan. On December 6, 2011, Judge James Peck confirmed this plan and the estate indicated its intent in a January 27, 2012, filing to distribute between $8.1 billion and $10.7 billion, with distributions commencing on April 17, 2012. Derivatives counterparties received between 10.36 and 32 cents on the dollar.[36]

The plan offered predictability and closure for creditors 40 months after the largest bankruptcy in the United States occurred. But it also subordinated the contractual rights the parties bargained for at the outset of the trading relationship to the valuation mechanic the Lehman Brothers estate developed and the creditors and bankruptcy court approved. The Lehman Brothers' plan inserted itself as the sole party, despite being the defaulting party, able to make the termination amount determination, arguing that it was well placed to ensure that its methodology avoided exaggerated and self-serving claims made by nondefaulting parties. In essence,

---

36. Lehman Brothers Holding Inc., Third Amended Joint Chapter 11 Plan Notice Regarding Initial Distribution, Exhibit A, http://www.dm.epiq11.com/lehman /Document, April 11, 2012.

Lehman Brothers argued that its counterparties' variance in the interpretation of the contractual methodology for the value of the terminated derivatives transactions added to the time and costs involved in settling the derivatives portfolio. Rather than continue to negotiate each derivatives transaction with its counterparties, Lehman Brothers wanted instead to substitute a new methodology, postcontract and postbankruptcy. As a general matter, courts are reluctant to interfere with the parties' contract unless certain circumstances such as mistake, duress, or other factors are present. But here, perhaps given the uniqueness of the circumstances, the estate's derivatives counterparties agreed to a contractual modification of their rights as a nondefaulting party, most likely in an effort to remove the uncertainty of payment and the duration of negotiation with the administrator.[37] In essence, then, Lehman Brothers' ordinary creditors were not overlooked at the expense of its derivatives counterparties. The derivatives counterparties effectively subsidized the amounts payable to the bankrupt bank's other creditors.

III. WOULD DODD-FRANK HAVE CHANGED THE SETTLEMENT OF LEHMAN BROTHERS' DERIVATIVES PORTFOLIO?

Ben Bernanke, chairman of the Board of Governors of the Federal Reserve System, and Timothy Geithner, Secretary of the U.S. Treasury, perhaps more than most of their predecessors, were policy

---

37. The big banks are Bank of America Corporation, Barclays PLC, BNP Paribas, Citigroup Inc., Credit Suisse Group, Deutsche Bank AG, Goldman Sachs Group Inc., JPMorgan Chase & Co., Merrill Lynch & Co. Inc., Morgan Stanley, Royal Bank of Scotland Group PLC, Société Générale, and UBS AG.

mavens well suited in many respects for the roles economic history thrust upon them. After all, Chairman Bernanke was steeped in the arcane details of the Great Depression, while Secretary Geithner spent 13 years at the U.S. Treasury in the 1980s and 1990s, followed by more than 5 years at the Federal Reserve Bank of New York, tenures marked by currency crises and a large hedge fund failure, among other events.[38] These two gentlemen were instrumental in crafting proposals for how the financial regulatory framework should be modified, focusing in part on the "opaque" nature of derivatives and connecting derivatives to bankruptcy. For example, on April 20, 2010, U.S. Treasury Secretary Geithner testified that "the market turmoil following Lehman's bankruptcy was in part attributable to uncertainty surrounding the exposure of Lehman's derivatives counterparties."[39] Secretary Geithner added that "in this regard, Lehman's bankruptcy highlights another flaw in our financial infrastructure: the opacity and complexity of the OTC [over-the-counter] derivatives markets. These products grew exponentially in the run-up to the crisis. The notional amount of outstanding credit default swaps grew from about $2 trillion in 2002 to over $60 trillion at year-end 2007. Because these trades are conducted on a bilateral basis, the market has very little visibility into the magnitude of derivatives exposures between firms."[40]

The Financial Crisis Inquiry Commission's report, among other sources, has already noted that the market turmoil following Lehman Brothers' bankruptcy was more likely connected with former Secretary of the U.S. Treasury Hank Paulson's unveiling of the Troubled

---

38. David Skeel, *The New Financial Deal: Understanding the Dodd-Frank Act and Its (Unintended) Consequences* 44 (John Wiley & Sons, 2011).

39. Testimony of U.S. Treasury Secretary Timothy Geithner before the Committee on Financial Services, U.S. House of Representatives, April 20, 2010.

40. *Id.*

Assets Relief Program and the $85 billion government bailout of AIG rather than the failure of Lehman Brothers and uncertainty about derivatives counterparty exposure.[41] Moreover, policy makers likely conflated or failed to appreciate the distinctions in the principal causes of failure of AIG (unhedged, noncollateralized credit derivatives trading), Bear Stearns (failure to sustain liquidity as a result of its reliance on the overnight repo market), and Lehman Brothers (poor risk management of its real estate portfolio and overreliance on overnight financing), thereby leading to policy conclusions that perhaps are unsupported by the complex reality of why those firms and others failed. Rather, policy makers focused on two objectives: (1) preventing or mitigating systemic risk when a major derivatives participant fails, and (2) granting regulators new resolution authority to prevent the government from bailing out the failing or failed firm. Policy makers accomplished these two objectives by: (1) crafting legislation in Title VII of Dodd-Frank that attempts to manage counterparty risk by requiring mandatory clearing of certain derivatives through a central counterparty and the consequent imposition of more uniform derivatives collateralization, and (2) introducing resolution authority in Title II of Dodd-Frank to address failed or failing covered financial entities with, among other businesses, a derivatives portfolio. Title VII is inextricably linked to Title II because the former aims to prevent or mitigate failure in the first place as it relates to derivatives, in part by enhancing information available to regulators, while the latter has

---

41. Financial Crisis Inquiry Commission, *Final Report of the National Commission* (*supra* n. 4), 356, 372. On September 15, 2008, when Lehman Brothers Holding Company filed for bankruptcy, the Dow Jones Industrial Average fell 4 percent, as contrasted to September 29, 2008, when the U.S. House of Representatives voted 228 to 205 to reject the Troubled Asset Relief Program and the Dow Jones Industrial Average fell 7 percent. *See also* Testimony of John B. Taylor before the Committee on Banking, Housing and Urban Affairs, U.S. Senate, March 17, 2011.

broad power available to regulators to take action to resolve a failed institution when such institution is deemed capable of introducing systemic risk.

A. Title VII—Derivatives Reform through Clearing and Collateralization

Title VII of Dodd-Frank requires that all eligible derivatives be cleared on a central clearinghouse, known colloquially as a "central counterparty" (CCP). Currently, a bilateral over-the-counter (OTC) derivatives contract is executed between two parties. The terms of that transaction and the amount of collateral posted in association with that trade are private. When a transaction is centrally cleared, however, this single transaction between a buyer and a seller is replaced with two transactions, each involving a third party, the central counterparty. In other words, the central counterparty is the buyer to every seller and the seller to every buyer, in essence standing between the buyer and the seller.

Clearinghouses perform a valuable function in their mitigation of counterparty risk. In order to do this, the financial resources of a clearinghouse must understandably be robust. The Commodity Futures Trading Commission (CFTC) proposed on October 1, 2010, that a clearinghouse must maintain financial resources to meet its members' obligations notwithstanding the default of one of its members with the largest exposures or the default two of its members designated as systemically important.[42] The CFTC also proposed that quarterly stress tests should be conducted to determine the amount of resources required. Given that JPMorgan Chase Bank,

---

42. *See* proposed CFTC Regulations 39.11(a)(1) and 39.29(a), http://www.cftc .gov. *See also* press releases at www.cftc.gov (October 1, 2010).

Citibank, and Bank of America are the three largest derivatives counterparties in the United States, the simultaneous collapse of two of those institutions could mean the termination of a $130.95 trillion notional derivatives portfolio—representing 18 percent of global notional derivatives value as compared to Lehman Brothers' estimated 5 percent.[43] The International Monetary Fund estimated that undercollateralization of derivatives relative to risks in the financial system may be $2 trillion.[44] The TABB Group estimates that near-term collateral requirements of moving interest rate and credit derivative transactions to a clearinghouse model will require an additional $240 billion in collateral.[45] It is uncertain whether the clearinghouses collectively will be able to address the magnitude of those figures through reserve funds and required collateral posting.

Policy makers were right to focus on collateralization as a risk-mitigation technique, as it is critical to the risk management of derivatives, both cleared and uncleared. However, collateralization of derivatives transactions has existed for nearly 20 years, so the posting of collateral to mitigate exposure is not new. Over time, the amount of collateralized derivatives exposure has increased as derivatives trading volume has increased. In 2000, there were estimated to be in place 12,000 International Swaps and Derivatives Association (ISDA) Credit Support Annexes, the principal document for derivatives collateralization.[46] By the end of 2010, the ISDA

---

43. OCC Quarterly Report on Bank Trading and Derivatives Activities, Third Quarter 2011, http://www.occ.gov/topics/capital-markets/financial-markets/trading/derivatives/dq311.pdf, Table 1.

44. Manmohan Singh and James Aitken, "Counterparty Risk, Impact on Collateral Flows and Roles for Central Counterparties," IMF Working Paper 09/173.

45. E. Paul Rowady Jr., "The Global Risk Transfer Market: Developments in OTC and Exchange Traded Derivatives," TABB Group (November 2010), 6.

46. ISDA Collateral Survey 2000, http://www.isda.org/press/pdf/collsvy2000.pdf, 1.

annual Margin Survey indicated that there were 149,518 collateral agreements in place, with 90 percent of those agreements being the ISDA Credit Support Annex.[47]

Before the economic crisis began, toward the end of 2006, the ISDA reported in its annual Margin Survey that the gross amount of collateral in use was $1.335 trillion, with 59 percent of mark-to-market credit exposure covered by collateral.[48] Note that the largest firms, including the largest U.S. commercial banks, held 80 percent of all collateral.[49] By the end of the third quarter of 2011, the OCC reported that banks held collateral against 86 percent of their exposure to other banks and securities firms, and 179 percent against their exposure to hedge funds.[50] The latter figure is high because it is market practice for banks to require the provision of up-front or initial margin from hedge funds in addition to securing any current credit exposure.

Collateralization by product area varies, but the overall amount of collateralization is very high (and has remained so for the last several years). For example, the 14 largest reporting firms in the ISDA's annual Margin Survey in 2011 reported that an average of 96 percent of credit derivatives trades were collateralized in 2010, whereas among the total of 83 firms responding to the survey, that figure was 93 percent. Interest rate derivatives at the 14 largest reporting firms are collateralized at 87.9 percent, whereas among the

---

47. ISDA Margin Survey 2011, http://www2.isda.org/functional-areas/research /surveys/margin-surveys/, 3.

48. ISDA Margin Survey 2007, http://www2.isda.org/functional-areas/research /surveys/margin-surveys/, 4. The ISDA Margin Survey covers U.S. and non-U.S. market participants. In 2007, for example, 25 percent of respondents were based in the United States, while 52 percent were based in Europe or South Africa. The OCC Quarterly Reports, by contrast, cover only U.S. national banking associations.

49. *Id.*

50. OCC Quarterly Report, Third Quarter 2011 (*supra* n. 43), 6.

total of 83 firms reporting to the survey, that figure was 78.6 percent.[51]

The type of collateral is important as well. Cash has long been the preferred form of collateral. At the end of 2006, for example, nearly 80 percent of collateral was cash, with U.S. dollars being 46 percent of the cash pool and the euro representing 28.8 percent.[52] By the first quarter of 2011, the OCC reported that approximately 79 percent of the collateral held by U.S. banks was in the form of cash (51.5 percent in U.S. dollars and 28.1 percent in other liquid currencies like the euro), while the ISDA figures—covering the United States, Europe, and Asia—reported that 81 percent of collateral globally was in the form of cash, with 36 percent of collateral received in U.S. dollars and 40 percent in euros.[53] U.S. Treasuries as collateral represented 2.3 percent and equity securities represented 0.9 percent in the OCC's report, while the ISDA's annual Margin Survey in 2011 reported U.S. government securities as comprising 4 percent of the global pool of collateral received and European Union member-state government securities representing 2 percent.[54] While policy makers focused on the lack of collateralization of AIG Financial Products' derivatives trading, surely these figures

---

51. ISDA Margin Survey 2011 (*supra* n. 47), 13.

52. ISDA Margin Survey 2007 (*supra* n. 48), 6.

53. OCC Quarterly Report, Third Quarter 2011 (*supra* n. 43), 6. ISDA Margin Survey 2011 (*supra* n. 47), 8. Note that the Federal Deposit Insurance Corporation (FDIC) published an article in April 2011 entitled *The Orderly Liquidation of Lehman Brothers Holdings Inc. under Dodd-Frank* in the FDIC Quarterly (vol. 5, no. 2), wherein the authors state on page 6 that collateral, especially lightly traded collateral, can exacerbate losses when there is a counterparty default. However, as the OCC and ISDA reports show, the vast majority of collateral is in the form of cash, so the conclusion in the FDIC paper does not seem to match actual collateralization techniques.

54. ISDA Margin Survey 2011 (*supra* n. 47), 8.

show that that was an outlier based on its profile then as a subsidiary of a triple-A-rated entity. In addition, there was so little collateral provided that was in the form of something other than cash or Treasury securities that it does not even make an appearance on either the ISDA's or the OCC's survey. In other words, the industry was collateralizing with cash as part of its derivatives risk-management program for close to two decades without needing Congress to tell it to do so.

What has shifted under Dodd-Frank is that the CCP's calculation of required collateral is substituted for the individual counterparty assessing its risks. As is done today, both initial and variation margin will be required. Counterparties to cleared swaps will be required to post initial collateral to the CCP based on the CCP's assessment of the risk profile of that transaction.[55] In addition, each day, the CCP will set the variation margin associated with each transaction by recalculating the value of the transaction and accordingly calling for or releasing collateral, ensuring that counterparties have neutral risk positions in relation to the value of the underlying asset. In other words, the goal is that the CCP receives margin payments every day from counterparties whose contracts moved against them to ensure that the CCP and those that participate through the CCP always have funds to satisfy their obligations under contracts.

---

55. As it relates to uncleared swaps, Dodd-Frank requires swap dealers and major swap participants to notify their uncleared swap counterparties of their right to segregate their initial margin with an independent third-party custodian. The CFTC's November 2010 and April 2011 proposals would require that the custodian be independent of both the counterparty and the swap dealer or major swap participant and that there be a written custody agreement between the counterparties and the custodian. The ISDA's annual Margin Survey in 2011 reported at page 10 that only 7 percent of collateral received is segregated with a custodian.

The posting of collateral is tied to how the derivatives transactions of a clearinghouse member that has become insolvent are handled. For example, LCH.Clearnet Group's contract and related rules state that upon the default of a clearing member, the clearinghouse may close out and terminate the cleared transactions and will not transfer such positions. CME Clearing and ICE Trust, in contrast, allow cleared transactions and associated collateral to be transferred to another consenting clearinghouse member.[56] Were Lehman Brothers to have been a clearing member of CME, for example, upon its insolvency, its $35 trillion notional derivatives portfolio (and associated collateral) would have been ported to another clearinghouse member. The concern in a marketplace where major participants— such as Bank of America, Citibank, and Morgan Stanley, among others[57]—were under attack means that the portability of Lehman Brothers' derivatives portfolio may not have allayed counterparty risk to the nondefaulting party population because arguably an equally unstable counterparty was receiving those transactions or a stronger clearing member may have rejected the transactions being proposed for transfer without some sort of government backstop for the unknowable counterparty risk being assumed.

In addition to the default rules, the treatment of a counterparty's collateral is important. The CFTC requested and received comments

---

56. *See* "Cleared OTC Interest Rate Swaps: Protecting OTC Market Participants through the Security of Centralized Clearing," www.cmegroup.com (August 2011), 12.

57. Federal Reserve chairman Ben Bernanke testified to the U.S. Financial Crisis Inquiry Commission: "If you look at the firms that came under pressure in that period . . . out of . . . thirteen of the most important financial institutions in the United States, twelve were at risk of failure within a period of a week or two." *See* Thomas Russo and Aaron J. Katzel, *The 2008 Financial Crisis and Its Aftermath: Addressing the Next Debt Challenge*, Group of Thirty, Occasional Paper 82 (2011), 11.

on three principal collateral protection models. The first is the futures model, in which the customer's margin is held by the futures commission merchant but segregated from the futures commission merchant's creditors. The collateral is commingled in an omnibus account with other fund managers. The collateral can be tapped by the clearinghouse if the futures commission merchant does not have sufficient collateral to satisfy the requirements of the defaulting customer. The second model, physical segregation, takes the opposite approach. Here, each clearing agent and derivatives clearing organization segregates for purposes of its books and records the cleared swaps for each individual customer and the associated collateral. Thus, each clearing agent and each clearinghouse maintains a separate individual account for each customer. A third model, legal segregation, operates the same as the physical segregation model, but would permit the clearing agent and clearinghouse to commingle the relevant collateral.

Further, there are challenges associated with a clearinghouse's approach to collateral calculations. Currently, in the over-the-counter derivatives market, a counterparty's collateral requirements are assessed based on its aggregate exposure across all products. For example, a hedge fund that had exposure to a particular security through its prime brokerage account could have its collateral requirements offset through a derivatives transaction. Central clearing, however, will make this cross-margining more difficult. Positions associated with different products are unlikely to be assessed margin in this more holistic manner, thereby resulting in end users posting more collateral in aggregate than currently. It would be worth understanding whether those entities required to post more collateral than at present are the same entities that present the most systemic risk.

Finally, collateralization is clearly a critical technique for reducing counterparty exposure. One of Dodd-Frank's goals was to reduce counterparty exposure, but practically speaking, the Act changed very little in terms of how collateralization operates both before and after Lehman's bankruptcy, setting aside the fact that a clearinghouse will determine collateral required for cleared trades. The authors of the Federal Deposit Insurance Corporation's (FDIC's) article (cited in footnote 53) also misunderstood how collateral is overwhelmingly provided in U.S. dollars with significant rates of collateralization among counterparty types—all designed to ensure the minimization of counterparty losses. As the OCC Quarterly Reports demonstrate, there have actually been very limited counterparty credit losses incurred from derivatives trading activity by U.S. banks. From January 1, 1998, to September 30, 2011, U.S. bank losses caused by counterparty defaults on derivatives were $4.1 billion—including Lehman Brothers.[58] Collateralization, again primarily posted in U.S. dollars, reduced U.S. banks' credit exposure to capital at the end of the third quarter 2011 to $114 million—a very small fraction of the gross notional outstanding of derivatives held at U.S. banks.[59] These are remarkably low figures, particularly given that more than 350 banks failed during this period, Lehman Brothers collapsed, and effective government takeover of Fannie Mae and Freddie Mac occurred. It is noteworthy that when considering the losses that did occur, most involved derivative products tied to subprime mortgage derivatives or counterparties such as monoline insurers. And Dodd-Frank did not specifically address these products or counterparty types (although, admittedly, few monolines exist today).

---

58. OCC Quarterly Report, Third Quarter 2011 (*supra* n. 43), Graph 5C.
59. *Id.* at Table 4.

B. Titles I and II of Dodd-Frank and the Resolution of Systemically Important Financial Companies

A regulatory triumvirate chorused for greater powers to resolve failing or failed financial companies and nonbank financial companies in the wake of Lehman Brothers' bankruptcy. As made clear by Chairman Bernanke's statement cited in the introduction to this chapter, it was his view that the U.S. Bankruptcy Code in 2008 did not protect the public's strong interest in ensuring the orderly resolution of Lehman Brothers, and that that failure resulted in substantial consequences to the financial system and to the economy. Sheila Bair, chairwoman of the FDIC, testified that "failing nonbank financial companies . . . could only be resolved under the Bankruptcy Code, further exacerbating the financial crisis."[60] The U.S. Treasury Department's Web site recently boasted that financial reform will "end 'too big to fail' and taxpayer-funded bailouts, so that average Americans will no longer have to pay the price for greed and irresponsibility on Wall Street."[61] While those statements may carry a certain political appeal, it is my view that Dodd-Frank does not significantly alter how a complex derivatives portfolio like Lehman Brothers' would be handled, even with the enhanced orderly resolution authority granted to regulators, nor does the legislation provide comfort that the U.S. government would not bail out a clearinghouse were it to default.

To put the resolution authority of Dodd-Frank into context, it is helpful to understand the definitional corrals of its Titles I and II. Title I of Dodd-Frank established the Financial Stability Oversight

---

60. Testimony of Sheila C. Bair, Chairwoman of the Federal Deposit Insurance Corporation, to the U.S. Financial Crisis Inquiry Commission (September 2, 2010), 1.

61. *See* www.treasury.gov/initiatives/wsr/Pages/wall-street-reform.aspx (March 17, 2011).

Council (the "Council"). Comprised of various financial markets regulators and chaired by the Secretary of the Treasury, the Council has a dual mission: first, to identify risks and to respond to emerging threats to the financial stability of the United States and its financial system; and second, to promote market discipline by eliminating the concept of "too big to fail." The Council is thus tasked with designating "significant bank holding companies" and "significant nonbank financial companies" that will be subject to enhanced supervision by the Federal Reserve Board. "Significant bank holding companies" are those entities with at least $50 billion in total consolidated assets and are automatically considered under Dodd-Frank to be systemically important. "Significant nonbank financial companies" are those designated as systemically important by the Council. Thus, it is possible that a "significant nonbank financial company" in fact is not necessarily systemically important.[62]

Title II of Dodd-Frank allows for the "orderly liquidation" of these financial companies. Title II's definition of "financial company" captures four general categories of entities: (1) bank holding companies, as defined in § 2(a) of the Bank Holding Company Act of 1956;[63] (2) nonbank financial companies (which include, as noted previously, nonbank financial companies that the Council has determined must be supervised by the Federal Reserve Board); (3) subsidiaries of entities included within one of the first two categories (excluding insured depository institution subsidiaries and

---

62. The FDIC stated that some Lehman entities may not have been systemically important and thus would have been subject to the Bankruptcy Code. It would then be possible that one Lehman Brothers entity would be subject to Title II, while another would not. *See The Orderly Liquidation of Lehman Brothers Holdings Inc. under Dodd-Frank*, 5(2) FDIC Quarterly 13 (April 2011).

63. 12 U.S.C. § 1841(a). *See also* Dodd-Frank § 102(a)(1).

insurance companies); and (4) Securities and Exchange Commission (SEC) registered brokers and dealers that are members of the Securities Investor Protection Corporation. The fact that an entity is a financial company is not enough for the federal receivership provisions of Title II to apply, however. To be eligible for the resolution authority to apply, the organization must be a "covered financial company." At the risk of further definitional contortions, a "covered financial company" is a financial company to which a systemic risk determination has been made by the relevant set of regulators.[64] In other words, if Title I of Dodd-Frank results in an entity being deemed systemically important, then if such entity is failing or has failed, the federal receivership provisions of Title II may or may not apply, depending on a second determination made at the moment of possible failure.

Procedurally, Title II requires the Secretary of the Treasury or the FDIC and the Board of Governors of the Federal Reserve System—or the SEC in the case of brokers or dealers, or the Federal Insurance Office for insurance companies[65]—to present a written recommendation stating whether a particular covered financial company presents systemic risk. At least two-thirds of the then serving members of the Board of Governors and the Board of Directors of the FDIC (or parallel agency) must approve the petition of systemic risk designation. The relevant regulators must prepare a written analysis of whether the financial company is in "default or

---

64. The FDIC and the Board of Governors of the Federal Reserve System recommend whether the federal receivership provisions will apply to a financial company, and the SEC and the Board of Governors of the Federal Reserve System make such a recommendation for brokers or dealers. The Secretary of the United States Treasury makes the final determination (Dodd-Frank § 203(b)).

65. Dodd-Frank § 203(a)(2).

danger of default." This is intentionally broad in its definition, covering circumstances such as a bankruptcy case that has been or likely will be commenced; the financial company incurring losses that will or are likely to deplete all or substantially all of its capital; the assets of the financial company being less than or likely to be less than its obligations to creditors; or the financial company that is or is likely to be unable to pay its obligations in the ordinary course of business.[66] The repetition of the phrase "likely to" gives the relevant regulator the ability to take action before a financial company actually files for bankruptcy. The written analysis must also set forth the effect that the bankruptcy of the financial company would have on the financial stability of the United States; evaluate whether any private-sector alternatives to prevent the insolvency exist; assess whether or not a bankruptcy case is appropriate for the financial company; and evaluate the effect of a federal receivership on creditors, counterparties, and shareholders of the covered financial company, as well as other market participants.[67] Once this analysis is submitted, the Secretary of the Treasury, in consultation with the president of the United States, must appoint the FDIC as the receiver for the financial company if the Secretary determines that in fact the financial company is in default or in danger of default; that its default would have a serious adverse effect on the financial stability of the United States; that no private-sector alternative is available to prevent the insolvency; that the effect of the federal receivership on the claims of creditors, counterparties, and shareholders is beneficial; and finally, that an "orderly liquidation" would avoid or mitigate adverse effects.[68] The Council received

---

66. Dodd-Frank § 203(c)(4).
67. Dodd-Frank § 203(a)(2).
68. Dodd-Frank § 203(b).

negative public comments on its January 18, 2011, draft and reissued a second notice of proposed rulemaking on October 11, 2011.[69]

In the case of Lehman Brothers, it seems almost obvious in hindsight that the Council would have deemed the investment bank to be systemically important as a nonbank financial company and therefore subject to enhanced supervision by the Federal Reserve Board and, possibly, the resolution authority provided for under Title II. The encyclopedic Examiner's Report, issued in March 2010, provides extensive details regarding the doubtful solvency of Lehman Brothers. Using Dodd-Frank's directive to regulators to consider whether the nonbank financial company was in default or in danger of default, the balance sheet assessment was one obvious avenue of inquiry, but perhaps of greater importance than capital to an investment bank is its access to liquidity. The "unreasonably small capital" test, relied upon by bankruptcy courts to avoid prepetition transfers, is a helpful tool because the test takes a broader view of risks, like liquidity, that are not necessarily reflected through the more traditional balance sheet assessment.[70] As the Examiner's Report notes, the unreasonably small capital test had two components: first, whether it was reasonably foreseeable that Lehman Brothers was at risk of losing access to the financing that it required to operate its business and to satisfy its obligations as they became due; and second, whether Lehman Brothers' liquidity stress tests were reasonably constructed.[71] The SEC's and the Federal Reserve Bank of New York's performance as it related to the evaluation of

---

69. A range of issues remain to be addressed in the Council's guidance, but the second notice of proposed rulemaking, unlike the original notice, incorporates uniform quantitative thresholds to determine the population of nonbank financial companies that will be subject to further review for systemic importance. *See* www.treasury.gov/initiatives/fsoc.

70. Report of Anton R. Valukas, Examiner (*supra* n. 9), 1643.

71. *Id.* at 1649.

the strength of Lehman Brothers following the failure of Bear Stearns in March 2008 would not be immediately reassuring. Given that Bear Stearns had collapsed in a matter of days when its liquidity sources dried up, Lehman Brothers met almost immediately with the two regulators to discuss the results of its own liquidity stress tests, in essence examining scenarios for declining funding. In its May 28, 2008, stress test report, for example, Lehman Brothers reported to its regulators that it survived the stress tests by a margin of more than $10 billion.[72] It took the Federal Reserve Bank of New York more than two months after Bear Stearns' failure to develop and conduct its own stress test and scenario analysis, which concluded that Lehman Brothers would fail in a "Bear Stearns"–type run on the bank by $84 billion.[73] Moreover, the SEC failed to recognize or enforce Lehman Brothers' requirement to be able to monetize its liquidity pool within 24 hours, as Lehman Brothers relied instead on a five-day test.[74] Finally, the derivatives business conducted by LBSF indicated that at May 31, 2008, and August 31, 2008, it held 0.41 percent and 0.44 percent, respectively, in terms of its ratio of equity to assets, characterized as borderline solvent.[75] Under Dodd-Frank, perhaps these types of strands of analysis would have led the regulators to conclude that Lehman Brothers was in danger of collapsing.

While the enhanced supervision powers designated by Title I should provide regulators with greater information about the largest and most complex entities, if one of those entities actually begins to demonstrate weakness or fails, then the Secretary of the Treasury will hopefully be working diligently to achieve a private-sector solu-

---

72. *Id.* at 1679.
73. *Id.* at 1680.
74. *Id.* at 1507–1508.
75. *Id.* at 1618, 1621.

tion (which will be challenging, particularly during a volatile market like that experienced in the fall of 2008). Further, the Secretary of the Treasury will be obligated to assess whether the Bankruptcy Code provides an appropriate framework in which to resolve the failed nonbank entity. These requirements in Dodd-Frank should result in virtually no change in the bodies of insolvency laws that would apply to the financial company, either because the failing financial company or key parts of it are absorbed by an acquiring company or the failed company's insolvency is handled, in part, under the U.S. Bankruptcy Code and/or the Federal Deposit Insurance Act. The application of the Bankruptcy Code and the Federal Deposit Insurance Act would mean that no bailout of the failing company occurs, thereby inadvertently solving the "too big to fail" problem at least as it relates to bank holding companies, banks, and certain nonbank financial companies.

As it relates to derivatives specifically, many of today's largest counterparties execute their derivatives transactions through their U.S. commercial bank. Banks have historically been excluded from the U.S. Bankruptcy Code,[76] and instead bank insolvencies were addressed under the Federal Deposit Insurance Act. Despite the underlying policy claim that derivatives were responsible, at least in part, for the economic crisis and the creation of systemic risk, the insolvency of a derivatives counterparty that happens to be a bank was largely unaffected by Dodd-Frank.

Banks dominate as derivatives counterparties. A recent OCC quarterly report on U.S. banks' derivatives activity noted that the five largest U.S. commercial banks represent 96 percent of the total banking industry notional amount of derivatives trading activity.[77]

---

76. 11 U.S.C. § 109(b)(2).
77. OCC Quarterly Report, Third Quarter 2011 (*supra* n. 43), 1.

The concentration of a small number of financial institutions in the derivatives market has not shifted much in many years, including prior to Lehman Brothers' bankruptcy.[78] The vast majority of this derivatives trading activity is focused on interest rate swaps: in the OCC's First Quarter Report in 2008, that figure was 79 percent, whereas in the OCC's Third Quarter Report in 2011, it was 81.5 percent.[79] Interest rate swaps are perhaps the least complicated derivative instrument, particularly as compared to the challenges historically associated with credit derivatives in terms of credit event triggers and settlement, the complex calculations and dependencies of equity derivatives, and the inherent volatility of commodity derivatives, so presumably there is less risk in trading interest rate swaps than other derivatives.[80] In addition, the OCC reports that 62 percent of the top five commercial banks' net current credit exposure is to other banks and securities firms, with corporates representing 32 percent, and hedge funds—the most overly collat-

---

78. In the OCC Quarterly Report on Bank Trading and Derivatives Activities, First Quarter 2008, the five largest commercial banks represented 97 percent of the total banking industry notional amount of derivatives trading activity. In order by notional, those institutions were JPMorgan Chase Bank, Bank of America, Citibank, Wachovia Bank, and HSBC Bank USA. In the OCC Quarterly Report on Bank Trading and Derivatives Activities, Third Quarter 2011, the five largest commercial banks in order by notional were JPMorgan Chase Bank, Citibank, Bank of America, Goldman Sachs Bank USA, and HSBC Bank USA. In addition, the number of insured U.S. commercial banks engaged in derivatives trading has remained relatively stable: at the end of the first quarter of 2008 there were 1,003 banks (at 7 of 2008 Report), whereas at the end of the third quarter of 2011, there were 1,088 (at 1 of 2011 Report).

79. OCC Quarterly Report, Third Quarter 2011 (*supra* n. 43), 9.

80. Credit derivatives represent 6.3 percent of the OTC notional amounts for U.S. commercial banks, while equity derivatives are 0.7 percent and commodity derivatives are 0.6 percent. *See Id.* Note that these figures shift slightly when considering the data collected by the Bank for International Settlements, as greater numbers of institutions are covered.

eralized group, as noted earlier—being a mere 2 percent of net credit exposure.[81]

Thus, our financial landscape is dominated by the world's largest banks, which in turn are among the world's largest derivatives counterparties. While these banks will be more closely regulated under Title I of Dodd-Frank, the way in which their insolvency would be handled would not differ meaningfully from the pre-Dodd-Frank environment, as those banks that are insured depository institutions will still be subject to the insolvency regime of the Federal Deposit Insurance Act.

Nonbank financial companies, just as with bank holding companies, are captured by the definition of "financial companies" under Dodd-Frank. Nonbank financial companies are defined as those "predominantly engaged in financial activities."[82] This phrase was already embedded in § 4(k) of the Bank Holding Company Act of 1956 and Regulation Y. The Federal Reserve Board issued a proposal to refine this phrase on February 8, 2011, stating that "predominantly engaged in financial activities" should be measured either by a revenue or an asset test. Specifically, it was proposed that "predominantly engaged in financial activities" means the entity either has consolidated annual gross financial revenues in either of its two most recently completed fiscal years of 85 percent or more of the company's consolidated annual gross revenues, or its consolidated total financial assets as of the end of either of its two most recently completed fiscal years is 85 percent or more of the company's consolidated total assets. Financial revenue or financial assets are those derived from or related to activities that are "financial in nature," or the ownership, control, or activities of an insured

81. OCC Quarterly Report, Third Quarter 2011 (*supra* n. 43), 6.

82. Dodd-Frank § 102(a)(4)(A)(ii).

depository institution or any subsidiary of such institution. "Financial in nature" ties back to § 4(k) of the Bank Holding Company Act and includes activities such as securities underwriting, dealing, and market making and engaging in financial and investment advisory activities. The definition would not include activities that are incidental or complementary to financial activities, such as trading in physical commodities. In other words, companies that are not predominantly engaged in "financial activities" cannot be designated as systemically important.

Under Dodd-Frank, LBSF as a nonbank financial company, would likely be captured as a financial company subject to Title I's heightened regulatory scrutiny. As it relates to Title II being applied to a nonbank financial company such as LBSF, the treatment of derivatives would remain largely unchanged from the application of the Bankruptcy Code pre-Dodd-Frank. Nondefaulting counterparties under § 210(c)(8) of Dodd-Frank remain able to terminate, close out, and liquidate their derivatives contracts upon the insolvency of a nonbank financial company such as LBSF with the application of a one-day stay[83]—with such approach largely mirroring that applicable to banks under the Federal Deposit Insurance Act for the past few decades.

There are a handful of differences, though, such as the Bankruptcy Code's accommodation of a rapid sale of the failing business (such as with the sale of Lehman Brothers' broker-dealer business to Barclays coincident with Lehman Brothers' bankruptcy), as compared to the FDIC's ability under Dodd-Frank to transfer assets to another entity or to establish a "bridge financial company" to succeed to selected assets and liabilities of the covered financial company. The issue of whether an institution could have been persuaded to

---

83. Dodd-Frank § 210(c)(10)(B)(i)(l).

take on board another institution's $35 trillion derivatives portfolio, as assumed by the FDIC, seems naïve.[84] The time to conduct due diligence on the derivatives portfolio would be virtually nonexistent in an insolvency situation, potentially exacerbated by financial institutions' antiquated technology platforms for storing data on the derivatives transactions.[85] The compressed time frame for making these decisions would make it difficult for an institution to distinguish between assets the assuming institution wanted versus those assets it did not. Moreover, any absorbed derivatives portfolio would represent significant risk to the assuming institution, not just in terms of blindness as to the construction of the portfolio across asset categories, but also potentially hampering the ability of the assuming institution to hedge effectively, or to be caught in conflicting hedges with the portfolio being taken on board. One only has to consider Bank of America's ill-timed acquisition of Merrill Lynch and its shaky mortgage-related securities business to know that thoughtful financial institutions in the future will be slow to take on a failing institution's derivatives portfolio.[86] Even if an institution took on board a failing institution's derivatives portfolio, counterparties to the assuming institution may not feel any more positively toward their new counterparty than their prior failing one, particularly in volatile markets, contrary to the FDIC's optimistic view. Rather, those counterparties would likely terminate their

---

84. *Orderly Liquidation of Lehman Brothers Holdings Inc.* (*supra* n. 62), 17.

85. Other aspects of Dodd-Frank, however, should help in terms of having accurate data and records on derivatives transactions, as clearing will address these historic failures of record keeping. Not all derivatives transactions will be subject to clearing, however.

86. JPMorgan Chase Bank absorbed Bear Stearns' $13.4 trillion derivatives portfolio in March 2008, but only after an attractive purchase price was struck, along with a Federal Reserve Bank of New York $29 billion backstopped guarantee.

derivatives transactions at the earliest opportunity, creating much the same situation that existed in the fall of 2008.

If a "financial bridge company" were established under Title II of Dodd-Frank to take certain assets and liabilities of the failed institution, that entity could only be in existence for two years, subject to three one-year extensions.[87] That may not be sufficient time to dispose of the assets and liabilities of the derivatives portfolio. While the FDIC has very broad powers as it relates to its decisions as receiver, a key distinction from the Bankruptcy Code's approach, Dodd-Frank does impose upon the FDIC the obligation to use its best efforts to maximize returns, minimize losses, and mitigate the potential for serious adverse effects to the financial system.[88] In order to satisfy those requirements, it may be challenging for the final settlement of derivatives transactions to occur in a more expedited time frame than what has occurred under the Bankruptcy Code process applicable to LBSF. The same painstaking transaction-by-transaction approach will still be required. At present, the Lehman Brothers estate and the administrator commenced distributions to LBSF counterparties on April 17, 2012—three and a half years following the bankruptcy. If the financial bridge company had been utilized for LBSF, that vehicle would only have 18 months left to achieve final resolution—feasible, but not certain, and dependent on the complexity of the derivatives portfolio at issue.

Regardless of whether a financial institution or a financial bridge company received the failed institution's derivatives portfolio, it is unlikely that the FDIC's contention that all of Lehman Brothers' general unsecured creditors would have recovered 97 cents on the

---

87. Dodd-Frank § 201(h)(2).
88. Dodd-Frank § 201(a)(9)(E).

dollar, excluding any guarantees, would result. As noted previously, under the framework, adhering counterparties to LBSF receive between 10.36 and 32 cents on the dollar. There is nothing in Dodd-Frank that would preserve or freeze the value of the derivatives portfolio at the time of insolvency—prices for the underliers will still move—making the FDIC's rather precise recovery estimate unlikely.

Banks, logically the most likely candidates for application of the type of orderly resolution provisions in Title II, have in fact been the least likely to experience failures due to derivatives portfolio losses. Rather, the largest failures of entities due to mismanagement of derivatives to date have not involved any U.S. banks but instead entities that are nonbanks. Some of the more spectacular derivatives-related failures include the municipality of Orange County in 1994, which lost $1.7 billion of the county's $7.4 billion investment portfolio; the hedge fund Long-Term Capital Management's loss of $4.6 billion in 1998; and AIG Financial Products, a dealer and subsidiary of AIG that operated with a $2 trillion derivatives portfolio, which is continuing to be unwound. Orange County would not have been captured by Title II given the unique legal treatment of municipalities. Perhaps Long-Term Capital Management would not have attracted regulators' attention in a 2011 landscape of thousands of hedge funds, as compared to 1998, and thus not deemed worthy of being liquidated under Title II of Dodd-Frank. AIG Financial Products most obviously would have been deemed systemically important and therefore subject to Title I's enhanced regulatory supervision. If AIG had been allowed to file for bankruptcy, the winding up of its derivatives portfolio in AIG Financial Products would have proceeded under the U.S. Bankruptcy Code much as it currently has. If AIG Financial Products had been subject to federal receivership under Title II of Dodd-Frank, then the derivatives portfolio would have been unwound in much the same fashion.

While it is possible that the resolution authority of Title II will in practice be of little to no effect for unwinding the derivatives portfolios of financial companies, particularly if no bridge company is established to transfer the derivatives portfolios to, the clearinghouses present an entirely different risk profile. The legislative mandate of Dodd-Frank to clear certain yet-to-be-specified derivative transactions has guaranteed that the largest global financial behemoths will concentrate risk at the central clearinghouses they each trade and clear through, and as noted earlier, collateral may be set too low to prevent a systemic effect if one or two clearing members or significant customers default. In fact, the Basel Committee on Banking Supervision proposed in December 2010 that the largest global banks hold additional capital against the risk that a clearinghouse defaults.[89]

Currently, the largest commercial banks are the clearing members of the leading clearinghouses, partly as a result of the significant financial resource requirements specified by each exchange. For example, ICE Trust U.S. LLC ("ICE Trust"), owned by Intercontinental Exchange Inc., is a limited purpose trust company that serves as a central clearing facility for credit default swaps. ICE Trust requires that its 14 clearing members, including four of the five largest U.S. commercial bank derivatives participants, have $5 billion in capital.[90] The CME Group, which clears credit derivatives and

---

89. Bank for International Settlements, "Capitalisation of Bank Exposures to Central Counterparties," http://www.bis.org/press/p101220.htm (December 20, 2010).

90. Rules of ICE Trust U.S. LLC, § 201(b)(ii).

interest rate swaps, has 10 and 12 clearing members for those respective products—again, with the largest U.S. commercial banks being clearing members.[91]

Section 804 of Dodd-Frank provides the Council with the authority to designate a financial market utility such as a clearinghouse as systemically important. As the Notice of Proposed Rulemaking in February 2011 stated, clearinghouses' interconnectedness concentrates a significant amount of risk in the market, and their payment and settlement processes are highly interdependent.[92] If the Council designated a particular clearinghouse as systemically important, then that clearinghouse would be subject to the provisions of Title VIII. The Notice on Proposed Rulemaking attracted 15 comment letters, but the comments were largely common to one another. In essence, these groups felt that in order to be systemically important, the type of market served by the clearinghouse, the nature and size of its counterparties, and the complexity and liquidity of the products should be considered in making the determination. In addition, consideration of the level of interdependence, whether the clearinghouse had the potential to create significant liquidity disruptions or dislocations in the event of failure, and whether the clearinghouse had the potential to create large credit or liquidity exposures relative to participants' financial capacity were also common themes.

The Council issued a final rule on July 27, 2011. It determined that there are several statutory considerations for the systemically important designation as it relates to financial market utilities

---

91. The CFTC revised a January 2011 rulemaking proposal on October 18, 2011, requiring $50 million in net capital. The CFTC also stated that a non–systemically important derivatives clearinghouse organization needed only enough funds to cover the default of its largest member.

92. 12 C.F.R. Part 1320.

("utilities") such as clearinghouses.[93] First, a two-stage process was established to evaluate whether a utility is systemically important, prior to a vote for such proposed designation by the Council. The first stage consists of a data-driven process that results in a list of utilities that may be systemically important. The second stage would subject the utilities on the list generated from the first stage to a more detailed review. For example, some of the criteria for consideration would include the number and value of transactions processed, cleared, or settled by the utility. Second, the aggregate credit and liquidity exposures to counterparties would be considered. For example, the mean daily and historical peak aggregate intraday credit provided to participants, as well as the value of the margin held would be assessed. In addition, an evaluation of the estimated peak liquidity required in the case of the default of the largest single participant would be considered. Third, the interdependencies and other interactions with other utilities or payment, clearing, or settlement activities would be examined. Finally, the Council would consider the effect that the failure of or disruption to the utility would have on critical markets, financial institutions, or the broader system. Under these criteria, the CME Group, ICE Trust, and LCH. Clearnet would be included, but it remains to be seen whether there will be other clearinghouses or other utilities that can be added to this list.

As noted previously, the clearinghouses have yet to finalize all their collateral formulations and their documentation for clients of clearing members. However, the rules of the leading clearinghouses have been published. In many respects, the rules resemble those of the well-understood ISDA standards, in fact with ISDA membership

---

93. *Id.*

being required.[94] The key difference, of course, is that unlike a privately negotiated derivative contract, cleared derivatives will have documentation that is truly standardized and therefore not capable of being modified by clients of clearing members.

There has been much industry thought given to how the default of a clearing member (or even the default of a client of a clearing member) will be handled, and waterfalls or priorities of payments are being finalized for the various clearinghouses. Sections 605 and 611 of ICE Trust's Rules provide that when a clearing member defaults, meaning that it or its guarantor has failed to meet its obligations or transfer requested collateral, the clearinghouse is permitted to terminate, liquidate, accelerate, and close out the client's "open positions." Section 805 of ICE Trust's Rules codify that bankruptcy and the failure to pay or deliver with respect to open positions or the guaranty fund are the only defaults applicable to ICE Trust itself.

Upon the default of a clearing member, ICE Trust's Rules provide that it shall determine the loss incurred and the amount of collateral that can be liquidated. Once the "closing-out process" has commenced, ICE Trust has three business days to decide whether it will replace all or part of the transactions of the defaulting clearing member by porting or transferring those transactions to other clearing members that will agree to accept their transfer. The client of the clearing member can decide (prior to default) to designate certain clearing members as acceptable parties to whom their cleared trades can be transferred in the event of a default.[95]

Thus, if ICE Trust or another clearinghouse were designated as systemically important, the termination of the defaulting party's

---

94. Rules of ICE Trust U.S. LLC, § 201(b)(viii).
95. *Id.* at § 20A-02.

derivatives transactions would in essence be transferred to another clearing member, with ICE Trust effecting such transfer within three business days. Collateral would be transferred along with the open derivatives position. The bankruptcy of such clearinghouse would depend upon the entity's organizational form and location.

C. The Automatic Stay under Dodd-Frank

Under the U.S. Bankruptcy Code and the Federal Deposit Insurance Act, counterparties to certain derivatives are generally permitted to enforce default and termination provisions in those contracts upon the insolvency of their counterparty. While the Bankruptcy Code does not impose a time frame for exercising those rights, the Federal Deposit Insurance Act allows such rights to be enforced after a one-day stay. In addition to those rights, the debtor's counterparties may also liquidate collateral that has been posted by the debtor. Any shortfall resulting thereafter will constitute unsecured claims against the bankruptcy estate, entitling creditors to share in any distribution.

Within weeks of Lehman Brothers' bankruptcy filing, Harvey Miller, the bankruptcy doyen tasked with the filing, testified that a "massive destruction of value" could have been averted if an automatic stay had been in place for derivatives contracts.[96] (Although interestingly, Mr. Miller remarked on December 6, 2011, that the provisions of the Bankruptcy Code resulted in "order evolv[ing] out of chaos.")[97] Derivatives counterparties' exemption from application

---

96. Testimony of Harvey R. Miller before the Committee on the Judiciary, Subcommittee on Commercial and Administrative Law, U.S. House of Representatives, http://judiciary.house.gov/hearings/pdf/Miller091022.pdf (October 22, 2009), 3.

97. "Court Confirms Lehman Bankruptcy Plans," press release issued by Lehman estate, http://www.nysb.uscourts.gov (December 9, 2011).

of the automatic stay, which has been embedded in the U.S. Bankruptcy Code since 1978 for an expanding class of products, was actually designed to achieve the opposite of what Mr. Miller asserted—the mitigation of systemic risk arising from cascading bankruptcies of other entities. By providing a safe harbor from the stay for these contracts, the delays assumed to be inherent in the bankruptcy process would be avoided and counterparties could reduce the losses that would otherwise result from the degradation of collateral pledged by the debtor.[98] Dodd-Frank did not alter the Bankruptcy Code's accommodation to derivatives. Rather, it continued with the 32-year statutory approach of allowing derivative contracts to be exempt from the automatic stay of action that applies to all other creditors. In Title II resolutions, Dodd-Frank followed the Federal Deposit Insurance Act in settling on a one-business-day stay.[99]

The arguments for and against the safe harbor for derivatives regarding the application of the stay have been sufficiently covered in academic literature. Once more in the legislative litany, Dodd-Frank essentially preserved the special treatment afforded to derivatives contracts. I believe the most salient factor in the debate has always been whether the safe harbor for derivatives manages to mitigate systemic risk. While in the view of the media and many policy makers, derivatives certainly continued to be characterized as weapons of mass destruction, the fact remains that derivative transactions were terminated quickly and efficiently, although obviously settlement of claims and the ensuing fiduciary requirements of administration certainly slowed the process. No major counterparties slid into bankruptcy, parties were eventually able to rehedge their

---

98. The President's Working Group on Financial Markets, "Hedge Funds, Leverage, and the Lessons of Long-Term Capital Management" (April 1999), 20.

99. Dodd-Frank § 210(c)(10)(B)(i)(I).

positions, and quality collateral was fairly ubiquitous both before and after the meltdown in 2008. While the period of the stay was debated in the negotiations that led to Dodd-Frank, it is my view that the imposition of a one-business-day stay is likely ineffective in terms of stabilizing the financial system, and barely provides the FDIC with enough time to identify an appropriate entity or entities to which the failed entity's derivatives portfolio could be transferred. What would be effective in mitigating systemic risk, however, is ensuring an expanse of time, ideally predefault, for a failing financial company to novate transactions or to establish a bridge bank for those transactions. In the post-Dodd-Frank world, the regulators on the Council cannot claim that inadequate powers stymied their risk-management efforts. The enhancements achieved in Title I of Dodd-Frank should of course ensure that Title II never comes into operation, and the application of a stay under resolution authority is thus superfluous.

IV. CONCLUSION

For all the hullabaloo about derivatives, their treatment in bankruptcy hardly changed under Dodd-Frank. Moreover, the experience of Lehman Brothers from a derivatives perspective demonstrates how quickly and effectively transactions can be terminated and how well a defaulting party postbankruptcy can manage and significantly increase the size of its estate. Certainly, the way in which these products will trade has been significantly altered under Dodd-Frank and these legislative refinements should lessen some of the risks presented by these products, most notably counterparty risk.

The practical reality, however, is that the inevitably growing interdependence of our financial systems and the participants within those systems make it likely that periods of instability will result. The challenge market participants and regulators will always face is minimizing the systemic effects of bouts of instability and preventing disruption in an "overnetworked" environment.[100] Dodd-Frank, while having little practical effect on how the largest derivatives counterparties will be treated in bankruptcy, hopefully achieves its potential through more effective and well-timed regulatory oversight. As Professor L. C. B. Gower once commented, the regulation and supervision of financial companies should not seek to achieve the impossible task of protecting fools from their own folly, but should be no greater than is necessary to protect reasonable people from being made fools of.[101]

---

100. *See* William H. Davidow, *Overconnected: The Promise and Threat of the Internet* (Delphinium 2011). With his background in electrical engineering and his decades of experience as a Silicon Valley executive and successful venture capitalist, Dr. Davidow offers an engaging read on the perils of being overconnected and how to minimize systemic disruptions.

101. L. C. B. Gower, *Review of Investor Protection: Report, Part I*, No. 9215 (Stationery 1984), 7.

PART C

LIQUIDATION AND REORGANIZATION

5

A Dialogue on the Costs and Benefits of Automatic Stays for Derivatives and Repurchase Agreements

Darrell Duffie and David Skeel

INTRODUCTION

For nearly two years, the two of us have had a running discussion on the costs and benefits of automatic stays in bankruptcy for qualified financial contracts (QFCs), particularly those held by systemically important major dealer banks.[1] Prominent among these QFCs are over-the-counter (OTC) derivatives and repurchase agreements

Duffie is at the Graduate School of Business, Stanford University. Skeel is at the University of Pennsylvania Law School. We are grateful for helpful exchanges with Marnoch Aston, Colleen Baker, Andrew Crockett, Doug Diamond, Richard Herring, Tom Jackson, Bill Kroener, David Mengle, Martin Oehmke, Ken Scott, Penfield Starke, Kimberly Summe, John Taylor, Paul Tucker, Bruce Tuckman, and Yesha Yadav. The views expressed here, however, are entirely our own, and need not be held by any of these commenters. Duffie has potential conflicts of interest that may be reviewed on his Web page, www.stanford.edu/~duffie/. Among these, he has been retained as a consultant by the estate of Lehman Brothers Holdings Inc. on matters potentially related to the subject of this chapter.

1. QFC is the term used for these contracts in banking regulation. The treatment in bankruptcy is similar in many respects, but the bankruptcy law does not have an umbrella term corresponding to QFC. It uses separate terms for different categories of QFCs, such as swap, repurchase agreement, securities contract, and forward contract.

(repos). Several large U.S. financial institutions now have aggregate notional positions in OTC derivatives exceeding $50 trillion.[2] Every business day, the broker-dealer affiliates of these same large banks roll over $100 billion or more of new repo financing of their securities inventories. As we later explain, in the event that such a large financial institution files for bankruptcy without automatic stays on these massive positions in derivatives and repos, its QFC counterparties would derive what amounts to significant additional priority over other creditors. The advantages and disadvantages of this priority, which we summarize here, have been a matter of significant debate for the past decade, particularly since the 2008 crisis.

This chapter, summarizing our cost-benefit discussion and recommendations regarding automatic stays for QFCs, focuses on one aspect of the resolution of systemically important financial institutions. In this sense, our inquiry is a narrow one. But the issues are enormously important. Almost any conversation or policy paper about the failure risks of extremely large financial firms eventually encounters the particularly tricky problem of safely transferring, terminating, or restructuring enormous portfolios of repos and OTC derivatives. Central to any treatment of this problem, which is discussed in several other chapters of this book, is the question of whether these contracts should be subject to an automatic stay. Although we are particularly concerned with this question as it relates to the Chapter 14 proposal developed by Thomas H. Jackson and advocated in this book, we also consider its implications for resolution under Title II of the Dodd-Frank Act.

Overall, we agree with each other on the nature of the advantages and disadvantages of stays on QFCs, but in some cases have

---

2. The latest available data can be found in quarterly reports of the Office of the Comptroller of the Currency.

weighed them differently in reaching policy judgments, such as what sorts of financial institutions and QFCs should be exempted from these stays. We hope that this report on our dialogue may shed some useful light on these trade-offs.

After some background on QFCs and automatic stays, we provide our joint analysis of the costs and benefits of stays on QFCs, with a focus on systemically important financial institutions, including the special case of financial market utilities. Following this, we state our respective policy conclusions. Briefly speaking, we both believe that repos (and certain closely related QFCs) backed by liquid securities should be exempt from automatic stays or receive an effectively similar treatment. Repos backed by illiquid assets, however, should not be given this safe harbor. We both believe derivatives that have not been centrally cleared should be subject to automatic stays. One of us believes that stays should also apply to cleared derivatives; the other favors an exemption of cleared derivatives from stays, except in the case of a failure of a regulated central clearing party. Largely, although not in every detail, our views are consistent with the treatment of OTC derivatives and repos proposed in the Chapter 14 bankruptcy treatment of systemically important financial institutions.

BACKGROUND

When a firm files for bankruptcy in the United States, a stay immediately and automatically goes into effect.[3] The stay prohibits a creditor from seizing or selling collateral, starting or continuing litigation against the debtor, or taking other action to collect what the

---

3. 11 U.S.C. § 362(a).

creditor is owed. In general, the stay has the purpose of giving the debtor breathing space and halting the destructive "grab race" that might otherwise ensue as creditors seek to collect what they are owed before the debtor's assets are exhausted. Creditors can negotiate with the debtor and other creditors, and can otherwise participate in the bankruptcy case. But they cannot terminate contracts or engage in ordinary collection activities without first obtaining the approval of the bankruptcy court. As a result of a series of legislative amendments in the three decades since the current framework was enacted in 1978, U.S. bankruptcy law now exempts QFCs from the automatic stay and several other core bankruptcy provisions (one of which, the preference provision, also figures in our following discussion). The exempted contracts include: swaps, which are broadly defined to include OTC derivatives and a wide variety of other contracts, as well as "any agreement or transaction that is similar" to any of the listed contracts; repurchase agreements; securities contracts; forward contracts; and commodity contracts.[4]

Derivatives are financial contracts whose payments are typically linked to the prices of other financial instruments. They are used mainly for speculation and hedging. Derivatives that are traded over the counter have an elaborate contractual regime of counterparty credit risk management that is based on collateralization of counterparty exposures and on the closeout netting of gains and losses on contracts with the same counterparty. An early termination closeout is triggered by events such as failure to pay, a change

---

4. The definitions can be found in 11 U.S.C. § 101(53B) (swap agreement); 11 U.S.C. § 101(47) (repurchase agreement); 11 U.S.C. § 101(25) (forward contract); 11 U.S.C. § 741(7) (securities contract); 11 U.S.C. § 761 (commodity contract). "Financial participant," another key term, is defined in § 101(22A). The clearing agreements that cover triparty repurchase agreements are a particularly relevant class of securities contracts, given the systemic importance of dealer banks, money market funds, and repo clearing banks.

of control, and, because of the exemption from the stay and related provisions, bankruptcy.[5]

A repurchase agreement, commonly known as a "repo," is a contractual arrangement under which a firm sells securities and simultaneously commits to repurchase them at a prearranged price on a given future date. Repos are used, among other purposes, to finance the purchase of securities. For this application, the cash received in the opening-leg sale of securities can be viewed as the cash proceeds of a loan; the repurchase price can be viewed as the loan payback amount. The securities act as collateral to the effective loan. The repo counterparty, who is the effective cash lender, holds the title to the securities during the term of the repo and can therefore protect itself from the failure of the effective borrower through its rights to the securities in lieu of receiving the cash back on the repo. Repos are also the most common vehicle for taking short positions in fixed-income securities. To create such a short, the counterparty immediately sells the securities that it receives at the opening leg of the repo. In order to meet its obligation to return the securities at the termination date of the repo, the counterparty buys them at that time in the spot market. The counterparty thus profits from any decline in the market value of the securities during the term of the repo. Shorts are used for both hedging and speculative motives.

As we have mentioned, the most important examples of QFCs for large dealer banks are OTC derivatives and repos. Securities

---

5. Derivatives and other QFCs also are exempt from bankruptcy's anti–ipso facto provisions. An ipso facto clause is a provision that defines the debtor's bankruptcy or insolvency as an event of default and thus grounds for terminating the contact. Derivatives counterparties can thus terminate their contracts when the debtor files for bankruptcy—see 11 U.S.C. § 559 (exempting repos from bankruptcy's invalidation of ipso facto clauses), § 560 (exempting swaps), and § 561 (exempting netting agreements)—whereas ordinary contract creditors cannot. See 11 U.S.C. § 541(c); § 365(e).

lending agreements are essentially the same as repos in most economic and legal respects, and are commonly used as a source of financing, to facilitate trade settlement, to take advantage of particular regulatory and accounting treatments, and as a step in creating short positions in equities.[6] Our remarks concerning repos can generally be applied to securities lending agreements, another prominent form of QFC.

The special treatment for QFCs, often called a "safe harbor," has been justified on a variety of grounds.[7] Safe-harbor proponents have argued that if derivatives and repos were subject to the automatic stay, then a debtor's failure could have a "domino effect," taking other market participants down with it. For example, a counterparty that had entered into a large derivatives contract with the debtor to hedge its business risks might find itself suddenly and unexpectedly unhedged. With a stay, it could not cancel its contract. It might not be able to enter into a new hedging contract on similar terms with another firm, and if it did enter such a replacement position, it would run the risk of having too large a total derivatives position if its original contract was unexpectedly assumed by the debtor's estate. The counterparty might also be harmed by the delay in obtaining access to its collateral, or if the market moved against it while the debtor was in bankruptcy. Any delay in the counterparty's ability to terminate its derivatives with the debtor

---

6. For an extended analysis of the similarities between repos and securities lending, *see* Andre Ruchin, *Can Securities Lending Transactions Substitute for Repurchase Agreement Transactions?* 128 Banking L.J. 450 (2011). For some of the uses and the institutional features of the market for securities lending, *see* Matthew Dive, *Developments in the Global Securities Lending Market*, Bank of England Quarterly Bulletin, Q3, 224–33 (2011).

7. The arguments summarized in this paragraph are described in greater detail in David A. Skeel Jr. & Thomas H. Jackson, *Transaction Consistency and the New Finance in Bankruptcy*, 112 Colum. L. Rev. 152 (2012).

could therefore destabilize the counterparty and might even undermine market confidence more generally.[8] Safe-harbor advocates have also warned about the ill effects of "cherry picking."[9] With a stay, a debtor could assume the contracts that are "in the money," while rejecting its bad contracts and relegating the counterparty's claim for damages to general unsecured status. The debtor's bankruptcy could therefore cripple certain counterparties, perhaps destabilizing the entire underlying market.

While QFCs are generally exempted from the automatic stay in bankruptcy, this exemption does not apply to the failure resolution process for regulated banks administered by the Federal Deposit Insurance Corporation (FDIC). Once the bank's primary regulator or the FDIC initiates such a resolution and the FDIC takes over as receiver, the bank's counterparties are prohibited from terminating their QFCs for up to 24 hours.[10] During this one-day period, the FDIC has the right to, among other actions, transfer QFCs to a bridge financial institution or reject them. A rejected QFC that is not secured by collateral would be treated as a general unsecured claim and relegated to the payout given to unsecured claims. If the rejected QFC were collateralized, however, the counterparty could immediately sell the collateral, reducing the amount it was owed; any deficiency would then be treated as a general unsecured claim. Historically, rather than rejecting QFCs selectively, the FDIC has usually assigned QFCs en masse to a bridge financial institution.

---

8. These arguments correspond to what is sometimes described as counterparty contagion and a confidence crisis.

9. *See, e.g.*, John C. Dugan, *Derivatives: Netting, Insolvency, and End Users*, 112 Banking L.J. 638, 640 (1995), emphasizing "cherry-picking" concern.

10. In the comparatively rare situation where regulators initiate a conservatorship rather than a receivership, there is a blanket prohibition on terminating QFCs or other contracts pursuant to an ipso facto clause.

Title II of the Dodd-Frank Act introduced new resolution rules for systemically important financial institutions (SIFIs). Although SIFIs are not precluded from filing for bankruptcy, regulators can put a SIFI into the new resolution framework if, among other conditions, it is in default or in danger of default and its failure could create systemic problems.[11] The Title II rules institute what amounts to a brief stay on QFCs that is in essence the same as the one-day FDIC stay applied to regulated banks. During the stay period of such a resolution, counterparties are not permitted to invoke the ipso facto clauses in their contracts.[12] In particular, they cannot terminate contracts until 5:00 p.m. of the day after the receivership is commenced. By that time, however, the contracts may have been rejected by the FDIC, or may have been transferred to a bridge financial institution or another acquirer of some portion of the debtor's business, without a right by the counterparty to terminate.

It is too early to tell which specific institutions will be subject to Title II resolutions. Major nonbank users of financial QFCs include central clearing parties for OTC derivatives, large hedge funds, large insurance firms, and large asset managers. Some of these could be designated as systemically important under the Dodd-Frank Act, which would make them candidates for Title II resolution in the event they fall into financial distress.[13] The Title II resolution process

---

11. The resolution requirements are set forth in Dodd-Frank § 203(b).

12. As noted earlier, an ipso facto clause is a provision that defines the debtor's bankruptcy or insolvency as an event of default and thus grounds for terminating the contract. Ipso facto clauses are standard provisions in OTC derivatives and repos.

13. Title I of the Dodd-Frank Act authorizes regulators to designate nonbank financial institutions as systemically important, and automatically puts bank holding companies with $50 billion or more in assets in this category. These institutions are subject to a variety of regulations—including higher capital requirements—that do not apply to other institutions. The Dodd-Frank Act does not make this status a prerequisite for Title II resolution, but it does require regulators to conclude that a

is to be administered by the FDIC in essentially the same manner as the resolution process for regulated banks.

Thus, U.S. law now applies what amounts to an automatic stay of approximately one day on QFCs held by banks, large bank holding companies, and designated systemically important nonbank financial firms. Central clearing parties for derivatives are, however, exempted from some aspects of the stay, whether or not they are designated as systemically important, under a special provision of the Dodd-Frank Act. We return to this limited exemption later. As for insurance firms, indefinite stays can be applied during insolvency processes in some venues, such as the state of New York.[14] In the European Union (EU), a series of "settlement-finality" EU directives offers exemption from normal bankruptcy holdups for QFC-like transactions.[15]

There has not yet been a "live-ammo" test of the application of stays on QFCs on the scale of the largest dealer banks or other major holders of OTC derivatives and repos. This absence of experience covers the history of FDIC bank resolutions and the Title II

---

financial institution's default could have systemic consequences as a prerequisite to putting the institution into resolution. Dodd-Frank § 203(b)(2).

14. For the case of insurance firms domiciled in New York State, see the discussion of § 7419 of the New York Laws in "How Safe is the Harbor? Navigating Restructurings Involving Insurance Company and Other Specialized Counterparties, CDSs, Mortgage Repos, Biofuels Contracts and Obscure Derivatives," ABA Business Bankruptcy Committee, Chapter 11 Subcommittee, September 25, 2008, Scottsdale, Arizona.

15. In "Systemic Liquidity Risk and Bankruptcy Exceptions," Centre for Economic Policy Research, Policy Insight Number 52, October 2010, Enrico Perotti lists the relevant EU directives. He writes: "The complete list is as follows: EU Financial Collateral Directive of 6 June 2002 (OJ L 168/43), the EU Settlement Finality Directive in 19 May 1998 on settlement finality in payment and securities settlement systems (OJ L 166/45), Directive 2009/44/EC of 6 May 2009 amending Directive 98/26/EC on settlement finality in payment and securities settlement systems, and Directive 2002/47/ EC on financial collateral arrangements as regards linked systems and credit claims."

process of Dodd-Frank, as well as resolution procedures used outside of the United States. Thus, some of our discussion of the failure consequences of stays is necessarily speculative. We have some experience with bankruptcy safe harbors, that is, with the *absence* of a stay, most dramatically in the Lehman Brothers case, but even here significant questions remain.

We subsequently explain how the behavior of systemically important financial institutions and their counterparties, both before and during failure, depends markedly on the presence or absence of an automatic stay. As a result, the existence of a stay has a direct and large impact on participants in these contracts, and may also have a major impact on financial market stability and thus the wider economy.

KEY COSTS AND BENEFITS

One of the reasons the two of us have spent so much time discussing safe harbors for QFCs during the past two years is that this exemption from the stay has costs and benefits that are both extremely significant. Potential losses that are purely transfers from one market participant to another are not necessarily significant to policy analysis on their own, but are important whenever there are net social costs, for example through systemic risk or deadweight frictional distress costs to the debtor or its counterparties. The social costs and benefits of these stays have been studied for some time.[16]

---

16. For recent analyses, *see* Mark J. Roe, *The Derivatives Market's Payment Priorities as Financial Crisis Accelerator*, 63 Stan. L. Rev. 539 (2011); Robert R. Bliss & George G. Kaufman, *Derivatives and Systematic Risk: Netting, Collateral and Closeout*, 2 J. Fin. Stab. 55–70 (2006); Patrick Bolton & Martin Oehmke, *Should Derivatives Be Senior?*, Columbia University working paper, May 11, 2011; and Franklin R. Edwards

QFC safe harbors could potentially raise social costs through five major channels: (1) lowering the incentives of counterparties to monitor the firm; (2) increasing the ability of, or incentive for, the firm to become "too big to fail," with the attendant moral hazard of relying on bailouts; (3) inefficient substitution away from more traditional forms of financing; (4) increasing the market impact of collateral fire sales; and (5) lowering the incentives of a distressed firm to file for bankruptcy in a timely manner. We now discuss these channels, and later turn to the similarly extensive potential benefits of the safe harbor.

The first and second channels are closely linked. As argued by Mark Roe (2010) and others, the safe-harbor exemption from stays reduces a QFC counterparty's incentive to monitor the debtor. Technically, the exemption does not give a derivatives or repo counterparty higher priority than other creditors, but by freeing a counterparty from the strictures of the stay that apply to most creditors, it has a similar effect. This protection diminishes the counterparty's incentive to carefully screen the debtor before entering into a QFC, in order to avoid exposure to weak debtors. The safe harbor also lowers the benefit of monitoring the debtor's financial condition during the term of the contract. Monitoring is beneficial to the extent that it disciplines the debtor from taking risks that are excessive or otherwise inefficient. Lowering the risk of the debtor's failure is a social benefit because of the deadweight costs of failure, such as legal expenses, lost franchise value, and potential knock-on costs to the financial system.

Even with a safe harbor, the incentive to monitor does not disappear, because a counterparty cannot be certain that it will be made

---

& Edward R. Morrison, *Derivatives and the Bankruptcy Code: Why the Special Treatment?* 22 Yale J. Reg. 91–122 (2005).

whole in bankruptcy if it is not fully collateralized. This was made clear in the case of Lehman's bankruptcy, which in some instances caused losses to derivatives counterparties above and beyond those associated with the normal performance of their derivatives positions with Lehman.[17] As explained by Kimberly Summe (chapter 4 in this volume), Lehman's large bank counterparties have recently settled about $22 billion in claims against Lehman for their losses on OTC derivatives, receiving between 27.9 and 39 cents per dollar of claim. From the reporting period following the failure of Lehman in 2008 until June 2011, U.S. bank holding companies have experienced approximately $12 billion in additional losses due to derivatives counterparty default, according to statistics compiled by the Office of the Comptroller of the Currency (OCC).[18] This belies the notion that QFC counterparties can walk away at default, paid in full, leaving only non-QFC creditors to bear the costs of bankruptcy. A significant quantity of OTC derivatives claims against Lehman remains unsettled to this day, more than three years after the bankruptcy. Nevertheless, the incentive for derivatives counterparties to monitor is certainly reduced significantly by the safe harbor. A similar dilution in monitoring incentives applies to repos.

The argument that safe-harbor prioritization lowers the monitoring incentives of one class of claimants relative to another mirrors familiar considerations that apply to ordinary senior and junior unsecured creditors. Creditor prioritization involves a well-studied efficiency trade-off, with the higher-priority creditor potentially decreasing and the lower-priority creditor increasing its monitoring.

17. Kimberly Summe, *An Examination of Lehman Brothers' Derivatives Portfolio Postbankruptcy: Would Dodd-Frank Have Made a Difference?* chapter 4 in this volume.

18. *See* "OCC's Quarterly Report on Bank Trading and Derivatives Activities, Second Quarter 2011," http://www.occ.treas.gov/topics/capital-markets/financial-markets/trading/derivatives/dq211.pdf.

Indeed, banks have sometimes been encouraged by regulation to issue subordinated bonds in order to improve monitoring. The argument was that the associated dilution of the monitoring incentives of senior creditors would be more than offset by the increased monitoring effectiveness of subordinated creditors, who would become the "canaries in the coal mine." Likewise, the fact that the safe harbor lowers the seniority of ordinary creditors relative to QFC claimants should improve the effectiveness of monitoring by senior unsecured creditors, at least for a firm that is not "too big to fail."[19] (Our consideration of the "too big to fail" effect follows.) Thus, the fact that the safe harbor has monitoring implications does not on its own imply a net loss of monitoring efficiency. In any case, if the loss of monitoring efficiency associated with the safe harbor involves a sufficiently large expected cost to a given firm, that firm could simply choose not to use derivatives. It could commit to avoid them by its charter or through debt covenants.

This trade-off argument does not apply, however, to the extent that the firm fails to internalize the costs of its failure to others. For example, if there is reason to believe that the debtor will be "bailed out" by the government before it collapses, the monitoring incentive of senior unsecured creditors is reduced. The likelihood of a bailout, moreover, grows with the size of the debtor's derivatives and repo books because of the systemic risk associated with large positions in these QFCs. A safe harbor from the automatic stay therefore allows, or even encourages, a dealer bank to operate bigger derivatives and securities businesses. Thus, the safe harbor contributes to the "too big to fail" moral hazard. This—the incentive to become

---

19. Some creditors, such as bank depositors, may be less likely to adjust their monitoring in response to the QFC priority. But these creditors do not predominate with the large financial institutions under consideration here.

"too big to fail"—is a second cost of the safe harbors from the automatic stay.

The third cost stems from the fact that the safe harbor may make repos and derivatives a cheaper source of financing than alternatives such as traditional secured loans. As evidence of this, a major expansion of the safe harbor for repos in 2005 may have contributed to a sharp increase in repo financing shortly before the 2008 crisis.[20] That a safe harbor increases the incentive to use one form of credit over another need not, on its own, be problematic. Basic Modigliani-Miller principles predict that a debtor that chooses to save money on cheaper financing with derivatives and repos would simply pay more for traditional debt financing because investors in bonds and loans who lose priority will charge higher interest rates in compensation for the associated increase in expected default losses. Absent frictions, such as the inefficiency that could result if traditional lenders are less effective monitors than derivative and repo creditors, there is nothing problematic about this. Even with frictions, a firm rationally chooses its all-in, lowest-cost form of financing. If extensive use of QFCs raises the firm's expected net frictional distress costs for itself and its creditors, in total, the firm would reduce its use of QFCs. (The costs to its counterparties and creditors is priced into the terms of its contracts, and thus borne by the debtor as well.) The firm does not consider the systemic costs of its financing policy, however, because it does not bear these costs. So, does the safe harbor cause a substitution away from other forms of financing that would have lower systemic risk costs?

Repos typically have shorter terms than traditional secured loans. The majority of repo financing is overnight; as a result, it is relatively

---

20. These changes extended the safe harbor to repos using noncash collateral such as mortgage-backed securities. *See, e.g.,* Stephen J. Lubben, *The Bankruptcy Code without Safe Harbors*, 84 Am. Bankr. L.J. 123, 138 (2010).

fragile. If repo lenders lose confidence in the debtor and refuse to roll over a debtor's repos, the debtor can lose access to this financing almost instantly, as occurred with the failures of Bear Stearns and Lehman.[21] With an automatic stay for repos, cash lenders might be less interested in offering so much short-term credit in the form of repos. Absent the safe harbor, some lenders such as money market funds that are subject to rules requiring ready access to their funds might also face regulatory obstacles to the use of repos. Would the next-best alternative form of financing be less subject to a run? It does seem likely that an automatic stay on repos would lower the attractiveness of short-term repos that are backed by relatively illiquid assets, such as collateralized debt obligations (CDOs). As argued by Gorton and Metrick, cash lenders may have viewed CDO-backed repos as a close substitute for cash deposits.[22] The safe harbor for QFCs enhances the ability of cash investors in these repos to quickly extract themselves at low expected cost from their credit exposures to weakening borrowers. Absent the safe harbor, a significant amount of precrisis repo borrowing backed by CDOs might not have occurred. This would likely have lowered some of the damaging systemic impact of the financial crisis. Going forward without the safe harbor, some of the borrowing by banks that is backed by relatively illiquid assets such as mortgages might have longer maturities and would perhaps occur in the form of covered bonds rather than repos. This could further lower the fragility of bank financing.

Fourth, in addition to promoting the financial fragility of systemically important borrowers, the safe harbor for repos could increase the potential for large and destabilizing collateral fire sales. With no

---

21. *See, e.g.,* Darrell Duffie, *How Big Banks Fail—And What to Do about It* (Princeton University Press, 2010).

22. *See* Gary Gorton & Andrew Metrick, *Securitized Banking and the Run on Repo*, 104 J. Finan. Econ. 425–451 (2012).

stay, repo cash lenders often have an incentive—and, in some cases, a regulatory requirement[23]—to sell the collateralizing securities they hold against repos as soon as possible after the failure of the debtor. The safe harbor, which provides an incentive for the use of short-term repo-based financing, might therefore lead to less stable markets.[24] The less liquid the collateralizing securities, the greater the adverse impact of fire sales on the underlying market.

Finally, the absence of a stay may diminish the willingness of the managers of a troubled financial institution to voluntarily file for bankruptcy. If the managers cannot stop counterparties from terminating their contracts and selling collateral, they are less likely to initiate insolvency proceedings because bankruptcy does not give them a mechanism for delaying termination. This makes it more likely that regulators will be left to initiate insolvency proceedings. Regulator-initiated insolvency could be more costly. Regulators have less information than the managers about the most efficient time to initiate insolvency proceedings; they may also hesitate for bureaucratic or political reasons, and may be more likely to rely on bailouts, which induce moral hazard.

Although we have focused principally on the exemption of QFCs from the stay, the associated safe harbor also shelters QFC counterparties from bankruptcy rules against "preferences." Under the ordinary preference provision, creditors are required to disgorge any payments or other transfers they receive during the 90 days before a

---

23. Under Rule 2a7, money market funds are not permitted to invest in many of the types of securities that back the repos in which they invest cash. For a discussion of the associated systemic risk, *see* A. Copeland, D. Duffie, A. Martin, and S. McLaughlin, "Policy Issues in the Design of Tri-Party Repo Markets," Working Paper, Stanford University and Federal Reserve Bank of New York, July 2011.

24. *See, e.g.*, Kenneth Ayotte & David A. Skeel Jr., *Bankruptcy or Bailouts?* 35 J. Corp. L. 469 (2009) (discussing bankruptcy's benefits and the effect of the safe harbors).

debtor files for bankruptcy.[25] (The preference provision is subject to a variety of exclusions, one of which is noted in the discussion that follows; the others are not relevant for present purposes.) The counterparties to a debtor's QFCs are exempt from the preference provision; they can retain any payments or collateral they have received on the eve of bankruptcy.[26] The preference provision that applies to other creditors has traditionally been justified as (1) promoting the equal treatment of similarly situated creditors, and (2) as discouraging creditors from grabbing essential assets when a debtor is in financial difficulty. With QFCs, this exemption from the preference provision has a potential chilling effect on the filing incentives of managers that looms as large as concerns about equal treatment or the antigrabbing concerns of preference law. If the normal preference provision applied, the debtor could retrieve any unusual payments or new collateral that it gave to a counterparty on the eve of bankruptcy, which would provide further incentive to file in some instances. (We say "unusual" because payments in the "ordinary course" are generally protected.)[27] If counterparties are exempt from the automatic stay, by contrast, the debtor does not have this option.

The collapse of AIG in 2008 vividly illustrates the implications. After AIG was downgraded, its previously uncollateralized derivatives counterparties began demanding that it post collateral. Goldman Sachs, for instance, made aggressive demands for collateral, leading to valuation disputes between it and AIG. These massive collateral transfers on the eve of AIG's collapse are classic examples of the kind of preferential transfer that could, absent the safe harbor for QFCs, be retrieved if the debtor filed for bankruptcy. Without

---

25. 11 U.S.C. § 547(b).
26. 11 U.S.C. § 546(e) and (f).
27. 11 U.S.C. § 547(c)(2).

the exemption for QFCs, the ability to retrieve this collateral would have given AIG's managers a strong incentive to file for bankruptcy as its fortunes deteriorated. Because Goldman and other counterparties were exempt from the normal preference rules, making recovery of the collateral considerably less likely, AIG's managers had much less incentive to use bankruptcy.

Although the costs of the safe harbors for repos and derivatives are considerable, they also bring some sizable benefits. The first is a reduction of the incentives of repo and derivatives counterparties to "run" as soon as the debtor's financial condition is suspect, accelerating a default or even causing a self-fulfilling expectation of default that need not otherwise occur. Even with the safe-harbor protection afforded by current law, QFC counterparties have demonstrated a tendency to run from a weakening debtor. This was the case with the failures of Bear Stearns and Lehman.[28] Absent the stay exemption, counterparties would have an added incentive to pull out at the first sign of trouble, lest their contracts with the debtor be tied up in a bankruptcy or other failure-resolution process. By giving counterparties greater flexibility to exit even after the debtor files for bankruptcy, a safe harbor for QFCs is likely to reduce the counterparties' incentives to run on the eve of bankruptcy. It is important to recognize that runs are not always undesirable. If a firm is insolvent and destined to fail, early intervention is likely to be preferable to delay, particularly if it reduces insolvency costs. In this context, a run can be seen as beneficial monitoring.

---

28. *See* Anton Valukas, "Lehman Brothers Holdings Inc. Chapter 11 Proceedings Examiner's Report," Volume 4, http://lehmanreport.jenner.com (2010); Duffie, *How Big Banks Fail* (*supra* n. 21); and Copeland, Duffie, Martin, & McLaughlin, "Policy Issues in the Design of Tri-Party Repo Markets" (*supra* n. 23). We note that derivatives contracts with a weakening counterparty can often be exited via novation to a new counterparty. A market participant could refuse to become the new counterparty, given the associated exposure to the failing original party.

But if the debtor is solvent, or if sudden exit will produce destructive systemic consequences, runs are undesirable. The exemption from the stay (and preference law) may make these undesirable runs less likely.

A second benefit of the safe harbor is that it increases the ability of a firm to rely on critical hedges. Dealer banks and certain other large financial institutions make effective use of high-volume and complex dynamic hedging strategies involving derivatives and repos. The imposition of an automatic stay, in the event that a financial institution's counterparty undergoes some form of failure resolution, could significantly impair the risk management of the financial institution or even destabilize it. Under a stay, derivatives and repos with the debtor would be in limbo until the debtor decides which contracts to assume and which to reject. This form of destabilization entails financial distress costs for the firm itself and additional costs to the economy at large if the firm is systemically important.

To consider this effect, suppose that a firm has a hedging transaction with a failing debtor. A stay might place the hedge in a precarious condition. Most obviously, a stay would allow the debtor to reject a hedging QFC whose gains had already offset losses for the counterparty. The very purpose of a hedge is to lower distress costs. A rejected QFC could therefore cause the counterparty to immediately experience distress costs. Further, the failed debtor's counterparty might be reluctant or unable to obtain a replacement hedge before it knows whether the debtor intends to assume the existing hedge. If a new "replacement" hedge is put in place and if it eventually turns out that the original hedge is assumed by the debtor, the combined effect of double hedging is about as risky as having no hedge at all. Conversely, if a new hedge is not taken, the counterparty might find itself unhedged if the debtor decides to reject the contract. To be sure, a counterparty could sometimes predict that a contract—such as an out-of-the-money swap—is likely to be rejected. But it often could not be certain, especially if market values were volatile. An exemption from the stay clarifies this situation, thus reducing risk. This lowers the potential distress costs of counterparties to the debtor, and for the same reason may lower systemic risk. Conversely, as we have already argued, an unlimited automatic stay on QFCs would likely lower the sheer volume of OTC derivatives and repos that are used in practice, eliminating much of the benefit of the improved performance of QFCs at failure that the safe harbor allows. Because of the safe harbor, counterparties terminated roughly 700,000 of Lehman's derivatives when it filed for bankruptcy. As explained by Summe in chapter 4, these terminations were processed without significant systemic knock-on effects. Similarly, Lehman's safe-harbored repos terminated as they matured with only moderate counterparty default losses. In the event that a debtor cannot perform at maturity, the repo counterparty is protected by its safe-harbored ability to liquidate its collateral.

Finally, safe harbors from stays reduce the risk of costly delivery gridlocks in securities markets that could otherwise occur at the failure of one or more systemically important financial institutions. Suppose, for example, that a failing debtor could limit access by its repo counterparties to collateralizing securities. If those securities are "trapped" in a stay, they cannot be used for the planned purposes of the repo counterparties. These planned uses include commitments to settle new securities transactions and to return securities to the counterparties of other repo agreements. It is not unusual, for example, for the outstanding quantity of commitments to deliver a particular on-the-run issue of U.S. Treasury notes to be several times the total outstanding issue size because of the chains of repos and other forms of pledges that are often made of the same securities.

A similar argument applies to securities lending agreements. In the absence of a stay, securities deliveries that are facilitated by repos and securities lending agreements can continue unimpeded by the failure of the debtor. To be sure, it can be argued that common knowledge of the existence of a potential stay on repos and securities lending agreements would change market practice in a way that reduces the quantity of such "fragile daisy chains" of delivery commitments, thus lowering concerns about significant delivery gridlocks. While this argument has merit, the ability to use QFCs to freely pledge and re-pledge securities generally promotes market efficiency. Indeed, central banks rely heavily on repos to promote market liquidity and to implement monetary policy. Further, as evidence of the systemic importance of the reliability of repo settlements, the U.S. securities industry has recently introduced a penalty for any failure to deliver Treasuries under a repo agreement, in order to lower the potential for costly settlement gridlocks and systemic risk.[29] This failure penalty is slated to be extended to other heavily traded fixed-income securities.

Tightness in the easily found supply of a given type of security reduces the likelihood that speculators and hedgers will be able to

---

29. *See* Treasuries Markets Practices Group, "Frequently Asked Questions: TMPG Fails Charge," September 23, 2011, where the TMPG writes: "Why does the TMPG recommend a financial charge on settlement fails? Persistent elevated fail levels create market inefficiencies, increase credit risk for market participants and heighten overall systemic risk. In higher rate environments, the time value of money that is lost when delivery is not made as contracted provides an incentive to sellers to deliver bonds as agreed. Given that this incentive is smaller in low short-term rate environments, sellers are less sensitive to the timeliness of delivery. The TMPG recommends a financial charge to provide an incentive to sellers to deliver securities in a timely fashion and to therefore reduce overall fail levels."

quickly and efficiently locate these securities for useful investment purposes.[30] The more liquid and active the type of security, the greater the social benefit of reliance on the unimpeded return of repo collateral. U.S. Treasuries are at the top of the list because of the size, efficient infrastructure, and "safe-haven" status of the cash and repo markets for treasuries. Thus, a discussion of the cost-benefit trade-off of automatic stays in repos could lead to safe-harbor policies that make a distinction among repos and securities lending agreements that is based on the importance of liquidity in the market for the underlying securities.

SAFE HARBORS FOR FINANCIAL MARKET UTILITIES

We turn now to a consideration of the special costs and benefits of stays on financial market utilities for QFCs, such as repo clearing banks and OTC derivatives central counterparties (CCPs).

A CCP, also known as a "clearinghouse," is a form of "financial market utility."[31] By "clearing" a derivatives contract, a CCP becomes the counterparty to each of the two original participants in the contract. That is, the CCP becomes the seller to each buyer, and the buyer to each seller. The main purpose of clearing is to insulate the original counterparties from counterparty default risk. The Dodd-Frank Act requires, with some exceptions, the central clearing of "standard" derivatives.[32] Roughly speaking, a "standard" derivative

---

30. *See* D. Duffie, N. Garleanu & L. H. Pedersen, *Securities Lending, Shorting, and Pricing*, 66 J. Finan. Econ. 307–339 (2002).

31. *See* Dodd-Frank § 803(6) (defining financial market utility).

32. Under Dodd-Frank § 723, the CFTC and SEC are instructed to review swaps and to determine which must be cleared. Exemptions will apply to certain market

is one that is sufficiently liquidly traded to be safely and efficiently cleared. Once the Commodity Futures Trading Commission (CFTC) and the Securities and Exchange Commission (SEC) interpret and implement this clearing requirement, some CCPs are expected to be extremely large holders of derivatives and to have large bilateral positions with essentially all major market participants. As a result, the question of whether and how stays should apply to a clearinghouse is now a crucial part of the equation.

Analogously, a single triparty repo clearing bank such as JPMorgan Chase and Bank of New York Mellon can have an intraday book of repo positions representing a significant fraction of the entire stock of important classes of fixed-income securities. Although ongoing reform of the triparty repo market has made some progress, significant systemic-risk concerns remain.[33] The goal for lowering the participation of clearing banks as intraday lenders to large dealer banks has not yet been reached. The ability to handle the default of a large dealer bank is uncertain. Other central repo-market utilities include the Fixed Income Clearing Corporation, Euroclear, and Clearstream.

The clearing agreements between a dealer bank and a triparty clearing bank are "securities contracts," a safe-harbored form of QFC. A standard bankruptcy stay on the QFCs of these sorts of financial market utilities could trigger significant damage to the

---

participants and types of trades. The most important of the exemptions under consideration is for foreign exchange derivatives. The U.S. Department of the Treasury has yet to finalize its proposed exemption of foreign exchange derivatives. If adopted, this exemption will apply to all requirements for "swaps" under the Commodities Exchange Act.

33. In its "Statement on the Release of the Tri-party Repo Infrastructure Reform Task Force's Final Report," February 15, 2012, the Federal Reserve Bank of New York, the relevant primary regulator, states that "the amount of intraday credit provided by clearing banks has not yet been meaningfully reduced, and therefore, the systemic risk associated with this market remains unchanged."

financial system. The situation could be compared to what might have easily happened following the notorious events at the World Trade Center in New York on September 11, 2001. As reported by Jeff Ingber,[34] financial market utilities for repos, including the Government Securities Clearing Corporation and the two main clearing banks, JPMorgan Chase and Bank of New York Mellon, were significantly incapacitated. Only extreme and highly discretionary human efforts averted a catastrophic market gridlock in the delivery of needed securities. Absent these efforts, many firms participating in these markets might have collapsed. In the end, there were approximately 2,000 failures to deliver promised securities, valued at about $96 billion.

Although a resolution authority could arrange for a failing debtor's repos or OTC derivatives to be "bridged to safety," and the contracts could be assumed in a bankruptcy, any uncertainty among market participants about the resolve and ability to do so quickly and effectively could lead to extreme and unsettling market behavior.

The applicability of the stay to financial market utilities is relevant in two different contexts: (1) in the event that one or more of the large counterparties to the central market utility default, and (2) in the event that the financial market utility itself defaults.

We first consider the case of default by a member of a derivatives clearinghouse. If such a debtor is put into resolution under Title II of Dodd-Frank, the clearinghouse is protected from the effects of resolution in several important respects. The receiver is explicitly required to continue to honor the debtor's margin and other obligations to the extent possible, for instance, and the CCP can terminate the QFC or exercise its other contractual rights if the receiver

---

34. *See* Jeff Ingber, *Resurrecting the Street: How U.S. Markets Prevailed after 9/11* (self-published, 2011).

fails to do so.[35] The clearinghouse does, however, face one major restriction: The CCP, like other counterparties, is subject to the provision that delays the exercise of termination rights until 5:00 p.m. on the day after the resolution is initiated.[36] The clearinghouse could insist on adequate margin during this period, but could not terminate unless the receiver fails to provide it. If the failing member's derivatives are bridged by the FDIC, they remain "alive" and unterminated, provided the CCP accepts the assignment to the bridge.[37]

Merely a short delay in the effective treatment of a failed clearing member's positions could be important in a setting of heightened market uncertainty. Even unfounded suspicions that a large CCP could be destabilized by its inability to quickly and efficiently terminate or transfer the derivatives of a large failing member could lead to extreme systemic risk. Under the current standards of the Committee on Payment and Settlement Systems and International Organization of Securities Commissions (CPSS-IOSCO), the default management plan of a CCP is to be designed so as to safely handle the failure of any two clearing members.[38] Under this standard, there is relatively low tolerance for unanticipated losses stemming from multiple failures of clearing members.

In order to mitigate some of the risks of a delay that might be induced by a stay, the CCP could, before the expiration of the stay,

---

35. Dodd-Frank § 210(c)(8)(G). In addition, if the receiver transfers a cleared derivative, the clearinghouse is not required to accept the transferee as a member. Dodd-Frank § 210(c)(9)(C).

36. Dodd-Frank § 210(c)(10)(B).

37. Dodd-Frank § 210(c)(9)(C) gives the CCP the right not to accept the assignment.

38. *See* Principle 4 of Committee on Payment and Settlement Systems, Technical Committee of the International Organization of Securities Commissions, "Principles for Financial Market Infrastructure," April 2012, Bank for International Settlements, http://www.bis.org/publ/cpss101a.pdf.

begin to plan for the termination or redistribution of the derivatives contracts that it holds with its failed member.[39] For example, the default management plan of ICE Trust, currently the largest CCP for credit default swaps, is based on an auction in which surviving members make bids and offers for the failed member's contracts. The auction could be conducted after one day has passed, if the FDIC has done nothing by then. The CCP could potentially call off the auction if the FDIC has assigned the derivatives to a bridge institution. Presuming no legal impediment, the CCP could even hold such an auction during the stay period, but with the stipulation that the executions of the auction trades are contingent on the expiration of the stay without an assignment action by the FDIC. Because the FDIC "stay" is a restriction on termination rather than a true stay, a contingent auction seems unlikely to violate the Dodd-Frank resolution rules. Conveniently, the FDIC is required to treat each failing member's derivatives positions with the CCP in an all-or-none fashion.

Clearinghouses are subject to the same rules as other parties with respect to QFCs in bankruptcy. Because of the safe harbors from the stay and from bankruptcy's anti–ipso facto provisions, the clearinghouse could immediately terminate the derivatives (as long as it does so relatively promptly) and hold or sell any collateral of a

---

39. Some CCPs manage the failure of a clearing member through termination settlement of the positions of the failing member rather than redistribution of the "live" positions to surviving members. Termination, however, implies that nondefaulting members who suffer unexpected and involuntary termination of their positions may suddenly be left without needed hedges. This could be destabilizing. For an auction-based approach that also allows for potential "haircuts" of nondefaulted cleared derivatives positions, *see* CDS Default Management Working Group, "Principles and Suggested Best Practices for Managing a Defaulted Clearing Member's Remaining Portfolio and a Shortfall in Available Funds," New York, January 14, 2011.

clearing member who has filed for bankruptcy.[40] For example, the CME clearinghouse liquidated its exchange-traded derivatives positions with Lehman rapidly, although not entirely without controversy.[41] The clearinghouse could not, however, unilaterally insist on margin adjustments. The exemptions from the stay and related provisions cover only the "exercise of any contractual right . . . to cause the liquidation, termination, or acceleration" of QFC agreements, "or to offset or net out any termination values or payment amounts."[42] The clearinghouse would therefore need to seek court approval of any requests for new margin. The clearinghouse also would be stayed from any efforts to collect any uncollateralized obligations that remained after netting and the disposition of its collateral.

The second possibility is that a clearinghouse itself, rather than one of its members, becomes financially distressed. Here, although the formal rules are similar, different factors may come into play. We start with the Dodd-Frank resolution rules. Although the statutory analysis is quite complex, CCPs appear to be subject to resolution under Title II if regulators make the appropriate determinations.[43]

---

40. In the Lehman case, the bankruptcy judge ruled from the bench that counterparties who delayed termination until months after bankruptcy was filed had waived their right to invoke the safe harbor from the automatic stay. *In re* Lehman Brothers, Inc., Case No. 08-13555 (JMP), Transcript [Dkt No. 5261], at 101–13 (Bankr. S.D.N.Y. Sept. 17, 2009). The ruling was appealed, but the parties later settled.

41. *See* Valukas, Lehman Examiner's Report (*supra* n. 28).

42. *See, e.g.,* 11 U.S.C. § 560 (swaps).

43. At first glance, it appears that CCPs are not subject to Title II resolution because they are explicitly excluded from the definition of "nonbank financial company" in Title I. Dodd-Frank § 102(a)(4)(B) (defining nonbank financial company). But (perhaps surprisingly) exclusion from Title I does not prevent a company from being subject to the resolution rules in Title II. Although large bank holding companies and nonbank financial companies that are designated as systemically important under Title I are the most obvious candidates for Title II resolution in the event of

As with the resolution of other financial companies, margin and other obligations presumably would continue to apply if a CCP were taken over under Title II. Counterparties would be subject to the one-plus day delay in exercising their termination rights.[44] In contrast, if a clearinghouse files for bankruptcy, counterparties of the clearinghouse would be permitted to terminate their contracts and take other steps to collect what they are owed by the CCP, as discussed earlier. Counterparties would, however, be required to seek court approval before taking any other actions, such as efforts to collect any uncollateralized obligations that remain after terminating a contract.

Although the formal rules are similar, the failure of a clearinghouse could pose particularly difficult issues for the resolution process. The danger of a run on a troubled clearinghouse exists because the first counterparties to terminate their contracts would likely be paid in full, whereas those that delay might be appreciably more exposed.[45]

The danger of a run on a CCP might be exacerbated by "interoperability" among CCPs, by which market participants have the op-

---

financial distress, the resolution rules are not limited to these firms. For the purposes of Title II, "any company that is predominantly engaged in activities that the [Federal Reserve] has determined are financial in nature" can be subject to resolution if its failure could cause systemic harm and the other requirements for invoking the resolution rules are met. *See* Dodd-Frank § 201(a)(11)(B)(iii) (definition of "financial company" potentially subject to Title II); Dodd-Frank § 203(b) (requirements for triggering resolution). It is not clear whether Congress contemplated Title II resolution of CCPs, which are subject to special treatment in Title VIII (including designation as systemically important under Dodd-Frank § 804), but they do appear to qualify.

44. Dodd-Frank § 210(C)(10)(B).

45. This is one of the points made in Julia Lees Allen, Note, *Derivatives Clearinghouses and Systemic Risk: A Bankruptcy and Dodd-Frank Analysis*, 64 Stan. L. Rev. (forthcoming 2012).

tion to clear a given derivatives contract in any of a set of related CCPs. Interoperability allows two market participants to enter a trade with each other and then clear the trade with two different CCPs. In this case, the two interoperating CCPs would have a master clearing agreement that, in effect, allows them to share collateral posted by their respective clearing members.[46] Given the requirement to clear, the absence of interoperating CCPs to whom clearing members can quickly "port" their positions could thus limit the potential for a run. Alternatively, with a stay, a run could be stopped once the failure resolution process or bankruptcy is initiated. Currently, there are no interoperability agreements among CCPs for over-the-counter derivatives.

At present, and probably for at least a few more years, J.P. Morgan, Bank of America, Goldman Sachs, Citibank, and Morgan Stanley hold a greater volume of derivatives, and far more complex derivatives, than most or all CCPs. The challenge faced by the FDIC in resolving the derivatives of a major dealer is thus currently greater than that for any CCP. This is also so because the legal and financial complexity of safely disentangling the QFCs from a failing financial firm would be much greater for a large global dealer bank than for a specialized central market utility such as a CCP. The concept behind the "living wills" provision of Dodd-Frank may help eventually, but the actual ability to safely handle the QFCs of a large dealer bank under a failure-resolution plan currently lags the concept, as emphasized by Summe in chapter 4. The number of entities that have OTC derivatives with a large dealer bank is enormous in comparison with that for a CCP.

---

46. *See* J. Maegerle & T. Nellen, "Interoperability between Central Counterparties," Working Paper, Swiss National Bank, 2011.

REPOS: OUR JOINT POLICY
CONCLUSION

Although the two of us tend to give somewhat different weights to the costs and benefits that we have described, we agree that these are the most important factors in assessing the usefulness of safe harbors. We also agree on one major piece of the puzzle: the basic treatment of repos. In our view, this treatment turns on the distinction between repos that are collateralized by highly liquid securities, on the one hand, and repos that are collateralized by less-liquid kinds of assets, on the other.

The value of a failing debtor's estate is not significantly enhanced by the ability to stay a repo counterparty's access to liquid collateralizing securities, such as Treasuries. Stays are designed to enhance the value of a debtor's estate through continued access to the sorts of assets or services that are critical either to ongoing business operations or to lowering frictional liquidation costs. Access to marketable securities might give the debtor a source of liquidity, which is of course essential for a financial institution, but this is the purpose of debtor-in-possession (DIP) financing. Indeed, if the failed debtor needs certain liquid securities, they can by definition be purchased quickly and at low transactional costs using DIP financing. Although DIP financing is not a perfect substitute for continued access to the securities since it must be bargained for and then approved by a court, a repo counterparty could not be forced to continue to lend to the debtor, *even without a safe harbor.* Under current bankruptcy law, lending contracts are automatically terminated when the debtor files for bankruptcy, and a promise to make a loan (defined as a "financial accommodation") cannot be enforced by the debtor.[47] A court would

---

47. 11 U.S.C. § 365(c)(2).

therefore be likely to lift the stay and to permit a party that is secured by liquid assets to sell the assets, or at the least to require that the secured party be fully protected.[48] Because liquid marketable securities are by definition easily converted to cash, and vice versa, there is no reason to delay a counterparty's access to them.

In summary, the more liquid the market is for a class of securities, the greater the expected efficiency gain of that market's continued reliance for liquidity on repo and securities lending safe harbors, and the lower is the likely benefit to failing debtors of a potential stay on QFCs backed by that class of securities. Because of this, one of us and our colleague Thomas Jackson conclude that repos of liquid securities should be deemed to be breached upon the bankruptcy of a debtor, giving counterparties immediate access to the pledged securities.[49] This is effectively the treatment afforded by a QFC safe harbor. We both agree with this conclusion, which is also reflected in the proposed Chapter 14 special bankruptcy provisions of Thomas Jackson (chapter 2).

A similar analysis would apply to the application of ordinary preference law to repos. In theory, payments or adjustments to a repo during the 90 days before bankruptcy would be subject to attack by the debtor or a trustee in bankruptcy as preferences. In practice, the danger to a repo counterparty of being forced to disgorge prebankruptcy payments or adjustments is limited. As long as the repo securities are worth more than the price at which the debtor is obligated to buy them back, any transfers by the debtor to a repo buyer would be protected. Payments to a fully secured creditor are not treated as preferential. This is based on the theory that the creditor would be

---

48. 11 U.S.C. § 362(d)(1) (providing relief from the stay "for cause," including a lack of adequate protection).

49. Skeel & Jackson, *Transaction Consistency and the New Finance in Bankruptcy* (*supra* n. 7).

paid in full even if no payments were made prior to bankruptcy, and thus is not being "preferred."[50] Repo buyers are essentially fully secured creditors. In other work, Skeel and Jackson have advocated that bankruptcy's "two-point net improvement" rule be applied to repos and derivatives, in order to remove any lingering uncertainty.[51] Under this rule, which is currently used for loans collateralized by inventory or accounts receivable, the counterparty would be protected as long as it was no more fully protected as of bankruptcy than it was 90 days before bankruptcy (or at the time the loan was made, if it was made less than 90 days before bankruptcy).[52] The same principle could be extended to repos. In our view, it makes sense to provide this protection to all repos, even those that involve relatively illiquid collateral.

To some extent, the safe-harbor treatment (for most purposes) of repos collateralized by liquid marketable securities, as opposed to less-liquid assets, is reflected in the current Bankruptcy Code, which does not treat certain "less liquid" forms of repos as qualifying for the safe harbor. Under the original definition, as adopted in 1984, only repos collateralized by Treasury bills and other cashlike securities were protected by the safe harbor. In 2005, the definition of repurchase agreements under § 101 of the Bankruptcy Code was expanded to include repos involving "mortgage related securities" as well as "mortgage loans" and "interests in mortgage related securities or mortgage loans."[53] The mortgage-related securities that were added to the definition in 2005 are often comparatively illiquid, as the

---

50. The secured creditor therefore does not receive "more than" it would have received absent the transfer, which means that 11 U.S.C. § 547(b)(5) is not met.

51. Skeel & Jackson, *Transaction Consistency and the New Finance in Bankruptcy* (*supra* n. 7).

52. 11 U.S.C. § 547(c)(5).

53. 11 U.S.C. § 101(47) (defining "repurchase agreement").

fallout from the 2008 financial crisis has made clear. The safe harbor further extends, under § 741 of the Bankruptcy Code, to a range of transactions known as "securities contracts" that effectively cover most of the remaining forms of secured lending currently conducted by dealer banks and clearing banks. We believe that this historical expansion of the repo safe harbor to include repos collateralized by less-liquid securities was probably excessive, at least from the viewpoint of social costs.

DARRELL DUFFIE'S POLICY VIEW FOR OTC DERIVATIVES STAYS

I believe that the safe harbor should be eliminated for all uncleared derivatives.[54] The transition to the loss of safe harbor for uncleared derivatives should be delayed for several years from its announcement in order to allow time for market participants to adjust their balance sheets and risk-management methodologies to an environment that includes stays on these contracts. There should be a comprehensive safe harbor for those derivatives that have been cleared by a failed market participant (other than a CCP) under a regulatory standard for clearing, such as Dodd-Frank in the United States.

This separate treatment of cleared and uncleared derivatives strikes a balance between costs and benefits, one that reaps the net benefits of reliance on a safe harbor where they matter the most, which is for large liquid classes of derivatives. This is basically the

---

54. The appropriate treatment of one important class of derivatives, foreign exchange (FX) derivatives, may depend on the pending decision of the U.S. Treasury Department regarding the clearing and other requirements for FX derivatives.

policy suggested by Tuckman,[55] who believes, however, that a CCP is not an appropriate approach to clearing. This separated approach to stay exemptions is only effective if a significant fraction of derivatives is cleared, and if those derivatives are essentially the most liquid. I think these conditions are likely to apply after some time has passed. This policy has the probable side effect of encouraging the use of clearing. While increased use of clearing could lower systemic risk, it is too early to be confident of that.

For the case of a failed CCP, as opposed to a failed clearing member, the cost-benefit trade-off for stay exemptions is more complex and depends in part on the potential for a run on a CCP. It is reasonable to suppose that the class of cleared derivatives largely coincides with the class of derivatives that is legally required to be cleared. If so, it would usually be illegal to run from a CCP to a counterparty that is not a CCP. However, there could be a rush to enter offsetting trades with a CCP before its failure. This would not likely destabilize a CCP that handles margins prudently, although it may lead to some disruption of related markets. After its failure, a CCP would presumably have the right to suspend the clearing of new trades, so a run via offsetting new trades could be stopped without a stay. Overall, then, the damage caused by a run on a CCP seems limited except perhaps in a situation involving interoperability, as we have explained. In the absence of a stay, I would propose a regulatory prohibition of the use of interoperability to novate derivatives from one CCP to another after the failure of one of the two CCPs, except as expressly permitted by the primary regulator of the failed CCP.

---

55. *See* Bruce Tuckman, "Amending Safe Harbors to Reduce Systemic Risk in OTC Derivatives Markets," Working Paper, Center for Financial Stability, April 22, 2010.

Aside from the effect of a run, one should consider the contagious effect of the failure of a CCP on its clearing members, and how that impact might be mitigated by a stay. By the very fact of its failure, a CCP is unable to meet its obligations to its clearing members in a timely fashion, whether or not there is a stay. How could a stay reduce the associated damage? Under the stay that would be accompanied by a Title II resolution of the CCP, the FDIC could use its discretion to separate clearing members into three groups: (1) those whose derivatives should be transferred (without recourse by the transferee) to a reliable "bridge CCP," (2) those whose derivatives should be allowed to terminate, be fractionally reduced, or be assigned to another clearing member under the normal contractual default-management process of the CCP, and (3) those whose derivatives should be rejected. If this discretion is used effectively by the FDIC, the stay could be a powerful mitigant of systemic damage caused by the failure of a CCP, including the total distress costs to clearing members. The main disadvantages would be any inefficient use of this power, and the effect of uncertainty among clearing members regarding how the discretion of the FDIC would be applied.

Under the new Chapter 14 of the bankruptcy law proposed in this volume, whether or not under a stay, a CCP that has filed for bankruptcy could provide some cash liquidity to clearing members against derivatives claims that are systemically important. This provision of liquidity would be subject to clawbacks described by Jackson, and could be funded through debtor-in-possession financing. During the stay proposed by Jackson, the debtor could also decide which clearing members would have their derivatives terminated or reassigned as stipulated under the original derivatives contracts, and which clearing members would have their derivatives rejected.

Absent a stay of derivatives with a failed CCP, the attempt to contractually terminate or reassign the derivatives of the CCP, nearly all of them simultaneously, could lead to indiscriminant and potentially uncontrollable damage to many clearing members. Confusion and uncertainty could be heightened among clearing members and more broadly. The contagion induced by an uncontrolled unwind is unpredictable.

The situation faced by a failed CCP can be compared to the failure of a major dealer bank, several of which currently have vastly more derivatives than any CCP, including more complex derivatives, and with more counterparties. With Lehman's bankruptcy, the systemic damage caused by the unstayed treatment of its OTC derivatives was manageable without heavy systemic damage, as explained by Summe in chapter 4, but this could in part be due to the other resources available to Lehman's estate. Given the absence of a stay, for example, Lehman's unsecured bond creditors offered a substantial loss-absorbing buffer to the derivatives claimants that would not be present for a failed CCP whose "waterfall" of margins, default-guarantee funds, and capital have, by the definition of failure, been fully exhausted. That is, there are likely to be little or no liquid resources available to a CCP once it has failed. The liquidity support of the Federal Reserve provided under Title VIII of Dodd-Frank is designed to offer cash loans collateralized by the noncash resources of the CCP. It might be only *after* cash liquidity supplied by the Fed has been exhausted that the CCP would fail (if it fails at all) and any stay could begin.

A decision by a government to "bail out" a CCP, providing it with new capital (as opposed to liquidity backed by the assets of the CCP), could mitigate systemic damage either before or after its failure. Such a bailout, however, could not be relied upon, especially in the prevailing political environment. In any case, reliance on this form of support raises moral hazard. It is doubtful that the cost-benefit analysis of stays for failed CCPs should place much weight, for policy purposes, on government bailouts.

Overall, I believe that it is prudent, pending further analysis, to allow a brief stay of the derivatives held by a failed CCP. The duration of the stay should be only long enough to allow the effective exercise of the powers allowed under the stay, assuming the existence of an efficient infrastructure for this purpose. For example, the stay duration of Chapter 14, three days, seems reasonable. Such a stay, however, would be too brief to make effective use of the stays absent effective information technology designed for the purpose of quickly exercising the powers allowed by the stay.

DAVID SKEEL'S POLICY VIEW

Although I prefer a short, across-the-board stay on derivatives in bankruptcy, as I detail in the discussion that follows, I quite like Darrell Duffie's proposal for a stay on uncleared derivatives. Such a stay would reach the derivatives that most need to be stayed; and as he notes, the differential treatment of cleared and uncleared derivatives would create at least a small additional incentive to use cleared derivatives. I also agree that the change in bankruptcy treatment should be phased in over time to minimize the disruption of shifting to the new regime.

I nevertheless believe that a short stay should be applied to all derivatives, cleared as well as uncleared. To be sure, several of the principal dangers of unstayed derivatives are most pronounced with derivatives that are not cleared. The risk of fire sales may be greater, for instance, since uncleared derivatives are more likely to be collateralized by illiquid collateral. But the collateral of cleared derivatives may also be illiquid, and even seemingly liquid collateral can also pose a risk of fire sales in the midst of a financial crisis. Similarly, a stay on derivatives may only give managers an incentive to file for bankruptcy rather than waiting for regulators to intervene if it (and ordinary preference rules) applies to cleared derivatives, since most dealers' derivatives portfolios will include large amounts of cleared derivatives.

Oddly enough, if Dodd-Frank achieves its objective of moving a large majority of derivatives to CCPs, imposing a stay on cleared derivatives may be more rather than less important. The likelihood that a substantial portion of a dealer's cleared derivatives will involve illiquid and difficult-to-value collateral will be much higher if there is a massive shift to clearing, for instance, and managers would have little incentive to prepare for bankruptcy if most of their derivatives portfolio consisted of cleared and therefore unstayed derivatives. To minimize disruption, I believe the stay should be short—Thomas Jackson and I have advocated a three-day stay elsewhere—but that it should apply to all derivatives. For similar reasons, I also believe that it should apply to the clearing bank in triparty repo arrangements. As Jackson and I have argued, the negative consequences of a short stay, and of generally applying the bankruptcy rules that govern other kinds of contracts, are likely to be much less significant than the derivatives industry fears.

If the stay did indeed include cleared derivatives, lawmakers would need to decide whether it should apply to the CCP as well as the debtor's counterparties, or just to the counterparties. There is a plausible argument for exempting the CCP from the stay. A three-day stay would complicate a CCP's margin calculations, since it would need to require adequate margin not just for current values of the derivative but also for potential changes in value up to three days into the future. But a CCP's margin calculations, under best practice, already are supposed to be enough to cover not only the normal remargining period but also the period necessary to unwind the position in a default scenario, which would take a few days.[56] Thus, a three-day stay would not significantly alter the CCP's time horizon. Similarly, CCPs would not be able to terminate and replace derivatives instantly, even in the absence of a stay. It would take the CCP a day or two to set up an auction to replace a debtor's derivatives positions. As long as the stay did not prevent the CCP from making preparations for the auctions, conditioned on the debtor's nonassumption of the derivatives (and I would advocate that the stay be defined to explicitly permit these kinds of preparations), I believe the effect of a stay on the CCP would therefore be limited enough to be manageable.

The failure of the CCP itself, rather than a dealer, would pose somewhat different issues. Some of the main objectives of resolving the financial failure of dealers and other firms do not apply in the same way to a CCP. With other firms, the desire to preserve the going-concern value of the business if it remains viable is an important consideration. This factor seems less central with a CCP. Limiting the potentially destructive effects of the inability to make good on large numbers of derivatives is a much more pressing consideration. In addition, it is not clear that the presence or absence of a stay would affect the CCP's managers' incentives to file for bankruptcy to nearly the same extent as with managers of a dealer or other firm.

The importance of a stay may depend on how many CCPs emerge, and whether the failing CCP has a large presence in the market. If a small CCP fails, the stay may not be essential. If a CCP of any size

---

56. *See* Committee on Payment and Settlement Systems, Technical Committee of the International Organization of Securities Commissions, "Recommendations for Central Counterparties" (*supra* n. 38).

fails, by contrast, I think a stay would be essential, for the reasons Duffie very persuasively details. Neither the FDIC nor a private decision maker could effectively handle large numbers of derivatives quickly enough to prevent systemic damage in the absence of the stay. It seems likely that the market for CCPs will be sufficiently concentrated as to warrant general application of a short stay to all CCPs, as Duffie recommends. The prospect of a stay might bring other benefits as well, such as encouraging derivatives users to make at least some provision for the possibility of a CCP failure.[57]

Overall, I differ from Duffie only in my conclusion that the stay should apply to both cleared and uncleared derivatives. I agree that the duration of the stay should be limited, and that it should be phased in over time. In my view, the imposition of a limited stay in bankruptcy would go far toward plugging a major gap in the Dodd-Frank reforms.

CONCLUDING REMARKS

After an extensive dialogue, and in part because of some convergence caused by that dialogue, the respective policy views that we have described are somewhat similar. To summarize, we both believe that repos (and related QFCs such as securities lending agreements) that are backed by liquid securities should be exempted from automatic stays, or receive an effectively similar treatment. Repos backed by illiquid assets, however, should not be given this safe harbor. We

---

57. Under the new Basel III capital rules, contracts that are centrally cleared are given a zero risk rating. This could permit financial institutions to externalize some of the costs of their risk taking to the CCP if the CCP does not charge its members the full cost of the risks that are transferred. The prospect of a stay could offset this effect to some extent.

both believe that uncleared derivatives should be subject to automatic stays. Skeel believes that stays should also apply to cleared derivatives. Duffie favors an exemption of cleared derivatives from stays, except in the case of a failure of a regulated central clearing party. Both of us believe that the period of any stay on cleared OTC derivatives should be only long enough for an efficient exercise of the debtor's rights under a stay, a few days at most.

6

The Going-Concern Value of a Failed SIFI

Dodd-Frank and Chapter 14

Kenneth E. Scott and Thomas H. Jackson

One of the principal objectives in a resolution of a failed systemically important financial institution (SIFI), as with any company, is to seek to maximize the remaining value of the firm and thereby reduce losses to its creditors or others. Thus, as the Federal Deposit Insurance Corporation (FDIC) put it in an article on "The Orderly Liquidation of Lehman Brothers Holdings Inc. under the Dodd-Frank Act":

> The keys to an orderly resolution of a systemically important financial company that preserves financial stability are the ability to [1] plan for the resolution and liquidation, [2] provide liquidity to maintain key assets and operations, and [3] conduct an open bidding process to sell the company and its assets and operations to the private sector as quickly as practicable.[1]

The point of the FDIC article is that Title II of the Dodd-Frank Act ("Dodd-Frank") provides a procedure much superior to the (existing) Bankruptcy Code, as shown by a hypothetical FDIC resolution of the failed Lehman Brothers investment bank.[2]

---

1. 5 FDIC Quarterly 1 (2011).
2. For an analysis of the hypothetical, *see* William F. Kroener, *Comment on Orderly Liquidation under Title II of Dodd-Frank and Chapter 14*, chapter 3 in this volume.

Prior to the adoption of Dodd-Frank, members of the Resolution Project had lengthy discussions about the "best" way to resolve large financial companies in financial distress. Goals included maximizing value for the claimants, minimizing systemic effects that were directly due to the distress or failure of a particular financial institution (rather than, say, caused by an event raising concerns about troubled assets held by a number of large financial institutions), and reducing the possibility of government bailouts that would distort market-based decision making and discipline.[3]

Out of this, the Resolution Project group set as a goal the development of a new Chapter 14 for the Bankruptcy Code, designed specifically for large financial companies, as the vehicle best suited to meet these goals. While Congress went in a different direction with its "orderly liquidation authority" in Title II of Dodd-Frank, we continue to believe the Chapter 14 solution has much in its favor. Thus, we continue to urge its adoption even if Title II of Dodd-Frank were to be left untouched.[4] But the FDIC article suggests that Title II of Dodd-Frank is, in fact, superior to bankruptcy, particularly as a vehicle for capturing going-concern value. We would like to test that, not against current bankruptcy law, but against bankruptcy law as we propose it with the addition of Chapter 14.

This chapter, accordingly, analyzes the ability of a modified bankruptcy law to meet the criteria given earlier and, specifically, its ability to preserve and maintain a financial firm's going-concern value. To begin, we consider the locus of value in such firms, using

---

3. Much of this work is contained in Kenneth Scott, George Shultz, & John Taylor, eds., *Ending Government Bailouts as We Know Them* (Hoover Institution Press, 2010).

4. *See* Thomas H. Jackson, *Bankruptcy Code Chapter 14: A Proposal*, chapter 2 in this volume.

Bank of America, Citigroup, and Lehman Brothers numbers as of the summer of 2008, when the financial meltdown was approaching its climax. At that point, the total book assets of Bank of America were $1.7 trillion, Citigroup $2.1 trillion, and Lehman Brothers $639 billion.[5]

I. WHERE IS THE VALUE OF A SIFI?

In looking at this, there are several categories of assets and revenues, both tangible and—also important (and often "off-book")—intangible.

A. Tangible (Other than Financial) Assets

Many firms (particularly manufacturing concerns) have substantial value in fixed assets: real estate, buildings, equipment, and other tangible assets that can be sold off separately to interested purchasers. If such assets are firm-specific (though often they are not), significant reductions in value may be incurred in a liquidation as opposed to a reorganization. However, for large financial companies such as we are focusing on, such tangible assets are—in contradistinction to manufacturing (and even retail) enterprises—likely to constitute a small part of the firm's value. We assume that a goal of maximizing the value of a firm will, with respect to a financial institution's fixed assets, rarely point either in the direction of a liquidation or a reorganization.

---

5. All data comes from Securities and Exchange Commission (SEC) 10-Q filings, available at http://sec.gov/Archives/edgar.

B. Securities and Financial Assets

For a commercial bank, loans are the largest part of its balance sheet (50 percent for the Bank of America, 35 percent for Citigroup), while for Lehman Brothers as an investment bank, other financial assets constitute practically everything that appears on a balance sheet. Consumer loans (mortgage, credit card, etc.) and commercial loans are difficult to sell off on an individual basis, which is why securitization pools have grown so extensively in recent years. But even asset-backed securities became illiquid in the 2008 financial panic, and institutions feared substantial losses from book values if they had to be sold into the market. The result was controversy over "fair value" accounting rules when they continued to be held on the balance sheet. Part of what is deemed "going-concern value" of a financial institution may be hard to distinguish from reluctance to recognize losses if the financial assets are sold into the market.

C. Revenues

Revenues may come from interest on loans and securities, or from fees (e.g., commissions), services (e.g., asset management or prime brokerage), and trading (e.g., dealing in swaps and derivatives). For the first half of 2008, Citigroup reported gross/net interest income of $58/28 billion, Bank of America $42/21 billion, and Lehman Brothers $17/1 billion. Noninterest income was $4 billion for Citigroup, $17 billion for Bank of America, and $37 million for Lehman Brothers.[6]

---

6. All reported trading losses on principal transactions: $12 billion for Citigroup, $1 billion for Bank of America, and $3 billion for Lehman Brothers.

D. Human Capital

Related importantly to the prior two categories, much of the value of financial institutions (albeit appearing nowhere on its balance sheet) is best thought of as its human capital. The future stream of noninterest income, in particular, depends upon "human capital"—the knowledge, expertise, and customer relationships of higher-level employees—which is lost if the firm does not continue in existence. Unlike other firm assets, however, the human capital can move on its own to other institutions (taking with it much of the firm's revenues as well). Keeping the human capital in place may be among the most important issues in resolving financial institutions in distress in a way that maximizes firm value, and among the most difficult to accomplish unless rapid resolution (and assurance) is provided.

E. Trade Names and Intellectual Property

Again related to human capital, proprietary trading practices and information databases, as well as the firm's name itself, may be significant contributors to a financial institution's going-concern value.

II. WHAT CAUSES A SIFI TO FAIL?

Failure, of course, has many potential causes. Some are firm-specific, such as poor management or fraud. But others are more systemic, and likely to affect—albeit to different degrees—a number of financial institutions simultaneously. In this category, in particular, two factors stood out in 2008: asset losses and creditor loss of confidence.

A. Asset Losses

In the financial meltdown of 2008, the primary driver was the end of a prolonged housing price bubble and a corresponding rise in defaults on subprime mortgages (characterized by low initial-rate loans with minimal down payments by borrowers with poor credit histories). Lender banks kept some of these loans on their own balance sheets, but transferred most in the form of asset-backed securities to institutional investors (including themselves) throughout the world.[7] As defaults mounted and asset-backed securities (ABS) ratings declined, large commercial and investment banks came to question the values that their counterparties were claiming on their balance sheets.

The function of capital is, of course, to cover unexpected losses and induce creditors to keep transacting with the firm. But leverage—the ratio of liabilities to capital—had become elevated in investment banks and suspect in commercial banks. The applicable capital requirements were proving to be inadequate to provide reassurance.

B. Creditor Loss of Confidence

As counterparties begin to become concerned about the riskiness of a firm they are dealing with, they undertake to reduce their exposure. Derivatives counterparties who are "in the money" demand more or better collateral, draining assets from the firm. (This was a particular problem that prompted government intervention in AIG.) Repo lenders may decide not to renew their transactions, which are usually very short-term. The result is that funding for the firm's normal operations disappears, and liquid assets that the firm

---

7. For a fuller account, *see* Kenneth Scott, *The Financial Crisis: Causes and Lessons*, 22 J. App. Corp. Finance 22 (2010).

can sell on short notice are insufficient to fill the gap. The firm's clearing bank may refuse to extend intraday credit in clearing and settlement, ending the firm's ability to engage in trading. In whatever form, the firm fails.[8]

III. RESOLUTION

With this in mind, we can now turn to an analysis of how Chapter 14's approach for resolving large financial institutions in financial distress is likely to fare. While our focus is primarily on Chapter 14, it is necessary to start with a comparison of Title II of Dodd-Frank, particularly in light of its claimed superiority to bankruptcy processes (albeit without the modifications we propose in Chapter 14). While many of the governing rules between resolution under Dodd-Frank and reorganization or liquidation under our proposed Chapter 14 of the Bankruptcy Code look similar (since, indeed, Dodd-Frank copied a number of bankruptcy's substantive provisions), there are also significant differences in procedures, and in some cases in overarching authority, that suggest the ability to maximize a firm's value will in fact be distinct between the two regimes. We start briefly with Title II of Dodd-Frank before turning our focus to the Resolution Project's proposed Chapter 14.

A. Title II of Dodd-Frank

While the statutory language of what became Dodd-Frank itself seemed focused on a liquidation rather than a reorganization

---

8. *See* Darrell Duffie, *How Big Banks Fail and What to Do about It* (Princeton University Press, 2010).

(through language such as a "receivership" or, indeed, the name of Title II itself: the "orderly liquidation authority"), the Boxer Amendment was intended to make the overarching goal of Dodd-Frank a mandate for a liquidation of a failed financial institution that enters its orderly liquidation authority under Title II. "All financial companies put into receivership under this title shall be liquidated," Dodd-Frank forcefully states.[9] "No taxpayer funds shall be used to prevent the liquidation of any financial company under this title." This liquidation mandate, although wildly divergent from the basic spirit of bankruptcy law during the past 100 years (which has had, if anything, a bias in favor of reorganization or rehabilitation), was a part of the spirit of the times respecting financial institutions in which Dodd-Frank was passed. In addition to the stern edict that the firm "shall be liquidated," it was also a part of Title II of Dodd-Frank that senior management was to be terminated (which would have been the case if the liquidation mandate were, indeed, followed).[10] Taken literally, these provisions would make the prospect of salvaging going-concern value through keeping together the things that create it for financial institutions—in particular, human capital, trade/intellectual property, and associated revenues—almost impossible.

---

9. Dodd-Frank § 214. Even the "purpose" language of § 204 focuses on the "authority to liquidate," to be done "in a manner that mitigates [financial stability] risk and minimizes moral hazard." Not a word is said about a goal of maximizing asset values.

10. *See* Dodd-Frank § 204(a)(2) (providing that "management responsible for the condition of the financial company will not be retained") and § 204(a)(3) (directing that "management" and "directors," among others, "having responsibility for the condition of the financial company bear losses consistent with their responsibility, including actions for damages, restitution, and recoupment of compensation and other gains not compatible with such responsibility"). *See also* Dodd-Frank § 206(4) and (5) (making such removal actions "mandatory" on the part of the FDIC).

Despite this seemingly inflexible liquidation mandate, buttressed by the provision of § 212 of Dodd-Frank that "[n]o governmental entity may take any action to circumvent the purposes of this title" (of which the required liquidation of a failed financial institution certainly sounds as though it qualifies), it is inevitable that regulators will rely on other, not entirely consistent, provisions in Dodd-Frank to restructure the firm via a merger, a sale of assets, or a transfer of assets to a "bridge financial company" (the latter being a putatively temporary company, but one that can exist for a long enough period so as to ultimately merge into yet another firm).[11]

Even this possible alternative, however, is not structured in a way easily designed to maximize values. The FDIC, being ill-equipped to manage a very large financial institution by itself (and recall, one of its first jobs is to ensure that responsible management has been terminated), is almost certainly likely to exercise these options in quick order, relying on its own judgment rather than the market.[12] Indeed, the determination of which parts of the financial institution warrant continuation and why, as well as the value of the assets and liabilities that are being sold or transferred, seem by Dodd-Frank to be left wholly to the discretion of the FDIC. Thus, even if one ignores the language of the Boxer Amendment, which seems probable, the structural obstacles put in place by the FDIC having to be the receiver attempting to run the business in the

---

11. All of these possibilities are at least open because of the language of Dodd-Frank § 210. *See generally* Douglas Baird & Edward Morrison, "Dodd-Frank for Bankruptcy Lawyers," 19 Am. Bankr. Inst. L. Rev. 287 (2011), also available at http://www.law.northwestern.edu/searlecenter/jep/symposia/documents/Baird_Dodd-Frank_for_Bankruptcy_Lawyers.pdf (making the point about the ability under Dodd-Frank to achieve a de facto reorganization).

12. A point persuasively made by David Skeel, *The New Financial Deal: Understanding the Dodd-Frank Act and Its (Unintended) Consequences* 149–50 (John Wiley & Sons, 2010).

interim (either directly or via the created "bridge" institution)—after discarding much of senior management with likely the largest human capital contributions to the institution—suggest that market-based valuations of any parts of the firm with a going-concern value will not be forthcoming.[13]

B. Bankruptcy under Proposed Chapter 14

A financial firm could file, under Chapter 14, either for liquidation or for reorganization. Consistent with a practice in existence since the equity receivership for railroads was invented in the nineteenth century, a firm that may have a positive going-concern value (or parts of it having such a potential value) will file in the first instance for a reorganization (Chapter 11 proceeding) under Chapter 14. In addition to the determination as to whether a firm is worth more as a going concern than liquidated, the bankruptcy process is focused on the determination of the value of assets, the value (and priority) of claims, and the distribution of the asset values to the claim holders in accordance with established priorities (known as the "absolute priority rule")—that is, secured creditors get paid first (up to the value of their collateral), unsecured creditors next, and various forms of shareholders last.[14] The question of how these com-

---

13. The requirement for wind-down plans may provide limited guidance to the FDIC as to parts of the business most likely to warrant continuation, even in the absence of market-based input as to values.

14. These rules are first set out in Chapter 7 of the Bankruptcy Code, notably §§ 725 and 726. In turn, they become the background rules for plan confirmation in Chapter 11, particularly via § 1126 (acceptance of plan), § 1129(a)(7) (nonaccepting claim holders must receive at least what they would have received in a Chapter 7 liquidation), and § 1129(b)(2) (for nonaccepting *classes*, the claimants are paid in full or no junior class receives or retains any property on account of the claims or interests of that junior class).

ponents interrelate, particularly in the context of a large financial institution, is the focus of the remainder of this chapter.

1. Running the Business Immediately after the Filing

While Dodd-Frank's orderly liquidation authority places the FDIC as receiver, and "requires" responsible management to be terminated, Chapter 14 (using the general rules of reorganization under Chapter 11) assumes that the "debtor" remains "in possession."[15] What this means, as a matter of common practice, is that the existing management of the firm continues to manage its operations, on the view that they have the best information about the firm's activities, as well as a sense of the valuable assets (including human capital). The notion is both that management presumptively has firm-specific knowledge (and value) *and* that a firm's financial distress is not inevitably the consequence of "bad management" (in the sense of management that was distinctly lower in competence and judgment than the management of other comparable institutions).

To be sure, management in some cases may not be ideal or may be too responsive to the old shareholders, and Chapter 11 (and thus Chapter 14) has a process for management to be replaced upon creditor (or also, in the case of Chapter 14, government) petition.[16] But the decision to replace management is both orderly and dependent on context (i.e., all things considered, is there a better manager?) rather than being a preemptive replacement of management by the FDIC as receiver. And with management (and other valuable employees—the firm's human capital) presumptively intact, the bankruptcy process can figure out, with the assistance of the constituent players (including creditors), what the likely best course is

---

15. Bankruptcy Code §§ 1101(1), 1107.
16. Bankruptcy Code §§ 1104, 1108.

for the assets—is it a continuation, a partial sale, or a liquidation? Continuation funding during this interregnum is possible because of the fact that postpetition financing is automatically entitled to administrative expense priority over preexisting unsecured claims,[17] and even higher priority can be given under certain circumstances, via the procedures in § 364 of the Bankruptcy Code.

2. Reorganizing or Selling the Assets

When the Bankruptcy Code was adopted in 1978, its structure (and history) suggested that the choice was either to "reorganize" and continue the firm under Chapter 11 or "liquidate" it under Chapter 7. Although the 1978 Bankruptcy Code originally structured itself around an idea of a "piecemeal liquidation" pursuant to Chapter 7, and a "going concern" reorganization pursuant to Chapter 11, events since that time have demonstrated that the two ideas are not as separate as originally conceived—and there are considerable advantages to a going-concern sale within a Chapter 11 reorganization.

For the first years after the enactment of the 1978 Bankruptcy Code, Chapter 11 reorganizations were ponderous events. The going-concern option—the reorganization—contemplated a process supervised by the bankruptcy court, but one in which the constituent players, through an adversarial system, argued about asset and liability values, and in which the "debtor-in-possession" had exclusive control over important parts of the process for long periods. The structure of Chapter 11 contemplated a debtor-in-possession who would have an exclusive period (presumptively, 120 days) in which to propose a plan of reorganization,[18] which would then be

---

17. Bankruptcy Code §§ 364, 503.
18. Bankruptcy Code § 1121(b).

voted on by the various classes of creditors and shareholders, with a bankruptcy judge overseeing the process, based on that judge's perception of the value of various securities given out in a reorganization and whether that satisfied the substantive tests ("best interests of creditors" for dissenting members in a class,[19] and "absolute priority rule" for a dissenting class[20]).

Even this description overstates the speed with which major reorganizations proceeded, as bankruptcy judges in the early years after the enactment of the Bankruptcy Code routinely extended the debtor-in-possession's exclusivity period for numerous reasons, including the difficulty of resolving disputed claims in time for Chapter 11's voting procedures that would follow upon the filing of a plan. In short, not only were markets (largely) not relied on, but the creditors (presumptively the new residual owners of an insolvent firm) found statutory obstacles in terms of real leverage over the future direction of the firm. This Chapter 11 process was often justly criticized as a mechanism for transferring value from creditors to shareholders through extended shareholder control over the firm and the reorganization process and plan, as well as inflated (or, at least, overly optimistic) judicial valuations, rather than focusing on maximizing firm values and allowing those values to be distributed according to the absolute priority rule.

Increasingly over time, however, the participants in a reorganization—including the bankruptcy judges overseeing the process—began to eliminate some of the worst abuses of the original

---

19. Essentially, whether the dissenting creditors would receive as much as they would have received "if the debtor were liquidated under chapter 7," Bankruptcy Code § 1129(a)(7)(A)(ii).

20. Essentially, that they are "paid in full," or a junior class "will not receive or retain under the plan on account of such junior claim or interest any property," Bankruptcy Code § 1129(b)(2)(B)(ii).

Chapter 11 process, principally by eliminating lengthy delay caused by extended exclusivity periods and by relying on market, rather than contested judicial, valuations of a firm's assets. Using the sale procedures of Chapter 3,[21] which originally had been contemplated largely for use in Chapter 7 (and for the disposal of "stray" unwanted assets in a Chapter 11), § 363 became the vehicle for going-concern sales of the entire business or major portions of a business. Such a procedure brought the market into play, with two significant consequences.

First, most of the ponderous delays in Chapter 11 could be avoided by a rather quick market bidding and sale procedure. The successful buyer of the assets (which could include creditors of the firm, particularly secured creditors, who could use their claims' value as a part of the purchase price), if it wished to continue them as a going concern, would put on them the appropriate capital structure, and the purchase price would become the new "assets" of the bankruptcy estate, to be divided among the nontransferred claimants according to the bankruptcy distribution rules. Disputed claims—unless assumed and transferred in the sale—did not need to be resolved prior to the sale, assets could be sold via market procedures, and the resulting "purchase price" could then be held by the bankruptcy estate while remaining claims' valuation issues were determined. Essentially, this allowed the assets (the business) to be severed from often complex and messy prepetition claims issues associated with the firm that had filed for reorganization. If claim valuation issues remained, they could be resolved without slowing down the process of selling the valuable assets to a new buyer in a market-based process.

---

21. Principally Bankruptcy Code § 363, providing for the "[u]se, sale, or lease of property."

Second, "distributional" valuation issues and disputes could be minimized when the proceeds of the sale consisted of cash and/or marketable securities. Importantly, such market valuations, via the sale proceeds, facilitated classwide voting and also determined the consequences of that voting. It was much clearer what value a dissenting creditor (or a dissenting class) would receive—a hugely valuable displacement of the disputes over value when a bankruptcy judge was making those determinations without reference to the market.

3. Reorganizations, Going-Concern Sales, and Financial Institutions

These features that developed since 1978—a quick, market-based bidding and sale—are essential cornerstones for Chapter 14 to build on as a viable process for reorganizing the nation's largest financial institutions, as we propose it should be. These market-based processes, in which a firm is run (often with existing management) while the appropriate response from market players helps inform a decision as to whether and how to sell the assets under § 363, has several key advantages for financial institutions. First, during the period following the filing, when the liquidity needs of the firm may be greatest, the sharp "severance" of prepetition from postpetition creditors encourages continuing dealings with the firm (through the receipt of administrative expense priority), unless the firm is perceived as badly insolvent and unlikely to be salvageable as a going concern. Second, markets and not the FDIC (or a bankruptcy judge) determine values—and, crucially, whether a firm's assets are worth more as a going concern or broken up and liquidated. Third, because the purchasers can be virtually any institution or group that can put together the financial package to enable the purchase, it is much less likely to lead—as does a bridge bank followed by a merger under Dodd-Frank—to increased concentration in an already-concentrated industry. Fourth, because the process involves market-based bidding for assets, and the receipt by the debtor in the Chapter 14 process of presumably marketable securities (if not cash) for the assets, it means that the valuation issues associated with the paying of nonassumed claims will themselves have a market-based foundation, making it much more difficult to have disguised bailouts than is the case in a bridge bank scenario.[22]

It is here where several features of the Chapter 14 proposal we have advanced join in order to ensure that bailouts taking place through a flawed sale under § 363 are minimized, as are other outright evasions of the legally clear priority rules enshrined in bankruptcy law. Those features include the ability to draw on the knowledge and expertise of federal agencies while, at the same time, minimizing the possibility that the experienced and independent Article III judges Chapter 14 contemplates will be subject to undue pressure by such a government agency to facilitate bailouts or other disruptions of preexisting priority rules.

To be sure, a government bent on a bailout can no doubt endeavor to accomplish it, even within the confines of (or in conjunction with) a Chapter 14 proceeding, but the transparency of a process overseen by an Article III judge, subject to clearly established legal priority rules and review by further Article III courts, can make this

---

22. The FDIC response to an earlier piece by Kenneth Scott suggested that this is overstated because, through the idea of continuing relationships, bankruptcy can (with reluctance, as the response acknowledges) sometimes "assume" obligations as postpetition administrative expenses (such as the decision by an automotive producer in bankruptcy to assume warranties of cars sold prior to bankruptcy). But this comes under a doctrine of necessity that requires judicial affirmation (and is subject to appeal). This seems almost certainly to be less "ad hoc" than would a comparable decision by the FDIC about which presolution obligations to favor because of "necessity."

more difficult to disguise (and is a major reason why we favor the use of Article III judges rather than bankruptcy judges—since the latter do not have the political independence that comes from lifetime appointment).

An instructive example is the Chrysler bankruptcy. In essence, apart from a couple of unwanted plants, the consequences of Chrysler's Chapter 11 bankruptcy filing were that all of Chrysler's assets were sold in a § 363 going-concern sale for $2 billion to a new entity (the "New Chrysler"). The assets received—the $2 billion purchase price—were all given to the senior secured creditors (who had claims of around $6.9 billion), thus satisfying, at least through the narrow lens of the Chapter 11 proceeding itself, the absolute priority rule. The buyers of the assets were, effectively, the U.S. and Canadian governments, which took a senior secured position in the New Chrysler for their cash contribution ($6 billion in total, of which $2 billion was used to "purchase" Chrysler out of the bankruptcy estate). Other securities against the New Chrysler were issued to Fiat (35 percent of the equity of the New Chrysler), to a new voluntary employee beneficiary association (VEBA) for retiree health-care obligations (a $4.6 billion note and 55 percent of the equity of the New Chrysler), and to the U.S. and Canadian governments (10 percent of the equity of the New Chrysler, in addition to the $6 billion senior secured position noted earlier—as well as some "upside potential" if the New Chrysler's stock price boomed). Warranties and the like, as well as obligations to most suppliers, were assumed; a number of dealership contracts were rejected (although a number of these rejections were later undone as a result of congressional pressure).[23]

---

23. Whether the meshing between state auto franchise laws and bankruptcy's executory contract provisions in § 363 permitted dealership rejections is a complicated question, not directly involved in this chapter's focus.

While structured as two distinct transactions, to satisfy the priority requirements of Chapter 11 (and to keep all of the issuance of claims in the New Chrysler outside of the bankruptcy process), collapsing the two transactions reveals a much less pretty picture in terms of legal rules and principles. In essence, the secured creditors, for $6.9 billion of claims, received $2 billion, while a group of unsecured creditors, far lower in priority—significantly, the retirees with future health-care benefits—received significant amounts of the New Chrysler. If (the old) Chrysler was, indeed, "worth" only $2 billion, then there should have been nothing of value to give to these retirees (or, for that matter, to Fiat, which added almost nothing constituting "new value" in any contractually enforceable sense).[24]

This was a rather shocking use of the § 363 sale process, as it allowed most of these "games" to be played outside of the bankruptcy process, in the New Chrysler, but in a way that surely shortchanged the secured creditors *in* the bankruptcy process.[25] The government would have run a significant risk that its desired bailout of the retirees (in particular) could not have been accomplished in a Chapter 11 reorganization through a true sale. Despite having a dollar majority of first secured claimants agreeing to the deal, the Chrysler that was subject to Chapter 11 might have lacked that class's acceptance of the plan (which requires both two-thirds in amount and 50

---

24. Fiat's 35 percent stake was for "access to competitive... vehicle platforms," "distribution capabilities in key growth markets," and "substantial cost saving opportunities." None of this sounds particularly "firm" in terms of committed new value. While the U.S. and Canadian governments did provide $6 billion to the New Chrysler, they were in fact given a senior secured claim for that $6 billion—so the $4 billion "kept" by the New Chrysler does not form the basis of the other securities given to Fiat or the VEBA.

25. *See* Mark Roe & David Skeel, *Assessing the Chrysler Bankruptcy*, 108 Mich. L. Rev. 727 (2009).

percent in number), particularly since the votes of Troubled Asset Relief Program (TARP) recipients might very well have been challenged as lacking "good faith," because of the federal government's pressures against these entities as the supplier of TARP funds.[26]

If so, under a plan of reorganization, the relevant test becomes not the "best interest of creditors" test under § 1129(a)(7), but the "absolute priority rule" as codified in § 1129(b). There would be almost no way to meet § 1129(b) without giving the secured creditors everything of value from (the old) Chrysler, including equity ownership in the New Chrysler that would result from the reorganization. It would have been very difficult to argue that the VEBA's note and equity interest in the New Chrysler were not being given "on account of" prebankruptcy unsecured obligations (retiree healthcare benefits). There would be similar questions about preserving prepetition warranty claims and prepetition trade debt in the New Chrysler (although some of these—continuing warranty claims— were more defensible than others for a continuing business). Finally, the bankruptcy judge overseeing a "traditional" Chapter 11 reorganization would have been challenged on matters such as whether

---

26. *See* Mark Roe, *A Chrysler Bankruptcy Won't Be Quick*, Wall Street Journal (May 1, 2009), at http://online.wsj.com/article/SB124113528027275219.html ("Worse, there could be a legal fight over whether the vote of Citibank and the other 'big four' creditors—J.P. Morgan Chase, Morgan Stanley and Goldman Sachs, who together hold 70% of Chrysler's debt—should be counted toward the two-thirds threshold that would bind the company's other 42 creditors. The Bankruptcy Code requires that the votes of creditors be given in 'good faith.' It won't be hard for the smaller creditors to argue that Citibank and other TARP recipient's votes aren't in full good faith. In agreeing to Treasury's offer of 32 cents for each $1 of their debt, the objectors would say, Citibank and some others were influenced by the fact that Treasury was keeping them afloat with federal subsidies. If this type of litigation begins, it won't be easily resolved."). *See also* brief filed on May 4, 2009, in the bankruptcy court of the SDNY by Chrysler's non-TARP secured lenders, http://www.scribd.com /doc/14952818/Objection-to-Chrysler-Sale-Motion.

Fiat's 35 percent equity interest in the New Chrysler was appropriate as an exchange for its "new value."

The end run in Chrysler's reorganization around the absolute priority rule and the rights of the senior secured creditors, and the bailout of others (such as retiree health-care benefits), was largely due to two factors. First, the bankruptcy judge nodded.[27] He permitted a condition to the § 363 going-concern sale being an understanding that any alternative bid would be "tested" against the requirements of the "government's" bid, including the receipt of claims against the New Chrysler of the retiree health-care plan.[28] And second, there

---

27. While the bankruptcy judge's opinion permitting the sale under the dubious procedures and restrictions was affirmed in a hasty decision by the Second Circuit, *In re Chrysler LLC*, 576 F.3d 108 (2d Cir. 2009) (argued on June 5, 2009, decided on June 5, 2009, with an opinion issued after the fact on August 5, 2009), the Supreme Court, on December 14, 2010, granted certiorari, vacated the Second Circuit's (and bankruptcy court's) opinion, and directed that the Second Circuit dismiss the suit as moot. *Ind. State Police Pension Trust v. Chrysler LLC*, 130 S.Ct. 1015 (2009). As a consequence, the Second Circuit's opinion has no precedential value. *United States v. Munsingwear*, 340 U.S. 36 (1950). This rather remarkable step—since the Supreme Court in July had issued and then lifted a stay, following the Second Circuit's ruling (and prior to the Second Circuit's written opinion justifying that ruling), allowing the sale to be consummated, 129 S.Ct. 2275 (2009)—has led some to speculate that the Supreme Court's vacating the Second Circuit opinion six months after the Court lifted the stay allowing the sale to go forward "was an expression of its disagreement with the Second Circuit's interpretation of the requirements of § 363(b)." Fred David, *Interpreting the Supreme Court's Treatment of the Chrysler Bankruptcy and Its Impact on Future Business Reorganizations*, 27 Emory Bankr. Developments J. 25, 27 (2010), found at http://www.law.emory.edu/fileadmin/journals/bdj/27/27.1/David.pdf. This is plausible, since at the time the Supreme Court lifted the stay and allowed the transaction to be consummated, the Second Circuit had not yet written its opinion explaining its reasons for affirming the bankruptcy judge's decision to allow the sale to go forward as then structured.

28. Assessments of competing bids included (1) whether the assets purchased are essentially the same; (2) whether the terms and conditions of the purchase would be "in substantially the form of the Purchase Agreement"; (3) whether the assumption "of any collective bargaining agreements" and entering into "the UAW Retiree Settlement Agreement" would occur; and (4) "any benefit to the Debtors' bankruptcy estates from the assumption of liabilities."

was also the real concern of a number of the secured creditors, who had themselves been recipients of TARP funds, that the government would be "all over them" if they engineered a higher competing bid—including by "bidding in" up to their $6.9 billion in secured claims.[29]

While there is little that Chapter 14 can do about the latter concern, it is designed to minimize the first concern: the undermining of market-based sales. It is our belief in proposing Chapter 14 that independent Article III judges, with the ability to hire experts to advise them, would not fail to see—and hence prevent—the kind of undermining of a true market-based sale (and valuation) that ultimately existed in Chrysler's case.

C. Systemic Consequences

While the focus of this chapter has been on the issues identified at the start by the FDIC's paper, we would be remiss in ending without at least mentioning issues of systemic consequences. Since bankruptcy (as currently fashioned) responds to the interests of the parties before it, it would perhaps seem to follow, almost *a fortiori*, that Title II's Orderly Liquidation Authority, conducted by the FDIC, would be better able to handle systemic consequences. We caution against reaching that conclusion for the following three interrelated reasons.

First, several of the proposals outlined in "Bankruptcy Code Chapter 14: A Proposal" (chapter 2), particularly the provisions involving

---

29. *See supra* n. 26. In an opinion earlier this year, the Supreme Court unanimously held that "going concern" sales under § 363 that did not permit the secured creditor to "credit-bid" violated the structure and spirit of the Bankruptcy Code. Radlax Gateway Hotel, LLC v. Amalgamated Bank, at http://www.supremecourt.gov/opinions/11pdf/11-166.pdf (May 29, 2012).

prepayments to existing creditors through debtor-in-possession financing and the direct "standing" to be heard and participate for the institution's primary regulator,[30] are designed to allow bankruptcy, as admittedly is not the case today, to deal directly with these issues. So, the comparison should be between Title II's Orderly Liquidation Authority and bankruptcy, *after* the addition of Chapter 14.

Second, as John Taylor (among others) has noted,[31] determining what constitutes a systemic consequence of the failure of an individual firm is very difficult. It is easy to think one sees "systemic" consequences, when all one really sees is correlation or access to new information. The issue, in terms of correctly identifying potential and dangerous systemic consequences, seems better handled in an adversarial system such as bankruptcy, overseen by a neutral judge who has statutory rules and principles to apply, than in a system overseen by regulators who may be under political pressure to "limit" the damages that might be forthcoming, not so much because of systemic risk as because of losses being suffered in a portion of the financial system that could (and should) be absorbed by the counterparties to those firms.

Third, and closely related to the second reason, is the question of which system is *both* better able to contain true systemic consequences *and* avoid bailouts. Under Chapter 14, as we have proposed it, it is difficult to bail out existing creditors of a failed firm,[32] forcing regulators to defend interventions that do so in a way in which they will find it harder to disguise discretionary bailouts of favored credi-

---

30. Jackson, *Bankruptcy Code Chapter 14* (*supra* n. 4), pp. 39–45.

31. John B. Taylor, *Defining Systemic Risk Operationally*, in *Ending Government Bailouts* (*supra* n. 3).

32. This is a consequence of the strictures for prepayments to existing creditors; see Jackson, *Bankruptcy Code Chapter 14* (*supra* n. 4), pp. 27, 39–45.

tors in the name of systemic risk. Again, we believe that the features that make a court venue so desirable in the first place—openness, transparency, judicial oversight, and appellate review based on established statutory rules and precedent—are promising also in distinguishing between avoiding systemic consequences and bailing out selected parties because they are politically influential or the regulator wants to avoid personal political risk.

IV. CONCLUSIONS

To summarize this discussion briefly, we return to the three criteria identified by the FDIC at the outset. The first is advance *planning* for failure and resolution. In the post-Dodd-Frank world, major financial companies are supposed to have prepared (and have approved by their supervisors) wind-down plans for going into bankruptcy. Since the past gives us only modest reason to have confidence that either managements or regulators will have correctly foreseen the source of the next crisis that comes along, and which operations or investments will be generating fears of insolvency, we should not rely too heavily on previously drawn up "living wills" to solve their resolution problems. Still, if the exercise improves the understanding of both managements and regulators with regard to the complexity of these giant firms, and perhaps leads to some simplification of their corporate structures, it could prove of value. But the value would be as great or greater in bankruptcy proceedings as compared to Dodd-Frank Title II, since the statute requires that the plans be designed with the former in mind.

The second criterion identified by the FDIC is *liquidity* to continue operations: to facilitate carrying on profitable aspects of the firm and endeavoring to minimize losses from unwinding the others.

Dodd-Frank gives the receiver the right to go to the Treasury at once for up to 10 percent of the book value of the firm's assets (and more later) with a priority claim against the estate, while Chapter 14 would provide that the debtor-in-possession (or trustee) could go to the market for such funds (also with a priority claim). If there is concern that in a financial crisis such funds could not be obtained even on that basis, the Treasury authority could, by statute, be extended in those circumstances, if needed.

The third criterion is an *open bidding* process to sell the company and its operations to the private sector. There are well-established rules and procedures to do this in bankruptcy reorganizations, including having unsecured creditors as bidders and thereby converting debt claims to equity and creating a solvent firm. The FDIC, acting as receiver for failed banks, has been accustomed to contacting a few other banks for a form of merger ("purchase and assumption"), in a process that has been far from open and transparent and results in the creation of still bigger banks. Indeed, with the very largest megabanks, it probably could not work at all. That is not to say that the FDIC could not possibly learn new tricks, but it clearly has no comparative advantage over bankruptcy for such a process.

Therefore, as we stated at the outset, we continue to urge adoption of a Chapter 14, even if Title II of Dodd-Frank were left untouched.

7

Dodd-Frank: Resolution or Expropriation?

Kenneth E. Scott

Much of the impetus for the financial reform legislation came from the view, correct or not, that when Lehman Brothers failed and had to go into bankruptcy, disaster ensued because it could not be taken over like a failed bank. Therefore, the Dodd-Frank Act ("the Act") in Title II created a new procedure ("Orderly Liquidation Authority") to seize even nonbank financial companies whose default would, in the view of the Secretary of the Treasury, have serious adverse effects on U.S. financial stability. This procedure gives unprecedented power and discretion to an administrative official, going far beyond banking law to the point of posing serious constitutional problems.

The Fifth Amendment provides that "No person shall . . . be deprived of life, liberty or property without due process of law," a clause at the heart of the rule of law that is the central pillar of our legal system. The meaning of "due process" in different contexts is something that English and American courts have developed over time to a reasonable degree of clarity. Usually administrative action to take someone's property must be preceded by notice and opportunity for a hearing.[1] If a court finds that summary action can be

---

1. The factors to be considered are discussed in *Mathews v. Eldridge*, 424 U.S. 319 (1976): the impact on the private party affected, the risk of administrative error, the governmental interest involved, and the value of additional procedural safeguards.

warranted by urgent circumstances, as the Supreme Court has held in the case of a regulator appointing a receiver or conservator for banks,[2] it has been premised on the availability of a prompt postseizure hearing. Thus, if the Comptroller of the Currency appoints a receiver or conservator to take over a national bank, the bank may go to district court for a full and open hearing "on the merits" of the asserted grounds.[3]

The Dodd-Frank Act squeezes preseizure due process down to the vanishing point. Consider how its resolution procedure is supposed to work. Companies "predominantly engaged" in financial activities are to be regulated and supervised by the Fed if they are systemically important. If the Treasury Secretary (upon recommendation by the Fed, and the Federal Deposit Insurance Corporation [FDIC] or the Securities and Exchange Commission [SEC]) makes seven determinations, including that a financial company is in danger of default that would have serious adverse effects on U.S. financial stability, he informs the company that he intends to appoint the FDIC as receiver. If the company does not consent, he petitions the district court of the District of Columbia (regardless of the location of the company's headquarters) for an order of authorization—and now the squeeze is on.

Under § 202(a) of the Act, the district court judge is given 24 hours from the moment of filing to (1) notify the company and hold a closed hearing, (2) review (limited to just two of the required seven findings) all the hearing evidence, (3) authorize the receivership or determine that the Secretary's action was "arbitrary and capricious," and (4) if the latter, provide a written statement of each reason supporting its opinion. If the judge cannot accomplish all

---

2. See *Fahey v. Mallonee*, 332 U.S. 245, 253–4 (1947).
3. 12 U.S.C. §§ 191(b), 203(b), and *see also* § 1464(d).

that in 24 hours, then the petition is deemed "granted by operation of law" and the receiver is to immediately begin liquidating the company (reorganization is prohibited by § 214). The decision and liquidation is not subject to any stay or injunction during the exclusive avenue of review: an appeal to the DC Circuit Court of Appeals or Supreme Court, whose scope of review is likewise limited to whether the Secretary's determination was arbitrary and capricious.

How would this work in practice? A financial company covered by the Act is by definition a large and complex institution, probably with hundreds of billions of dollars in assets. A large portion of those assets would consist of corporate or hedge fund loans, derivatives contracts, complex securities, and other financial contracts—much of them illiquid and thinly traded at best. That makes their valuation difficult and judgmental, as the argument over collateral between AIG and Goldman Sachs in January 2008 vividly illustrated.[4] The key determination by the Secretary is that the financial company is in danger of default. If a company has assets less than its obligations, is unable to pay its obligations in the normal course of business, or is likely to incur losses that will deplete substantially all of its capital, then it meets the definition of "default."[5] Asset valuations are likely to be at the heart of any dispute, and they will not be clear-cut.

Judicial review of administrative actions is a central safeguard against both error and abuse of power. Here, the judicial hearing before the seizure is designedly just about meaningless. Suppose the Secretary takes his action at the close of a business day, as has become customary in banking. He files with the petition an extensive

---

4. *See* Goldman Sachs, http://www.goldmansachs.com/media-relations/comments-and-responses/archive/response-to-fcic-folder/valuation-and-pricing.pdf.

5. § 202(c)(4).

set of documents prepared by the Fed and the FDIC or SEC for their recommendations and by Treasury staff for his determinations. By the next morning, the company has to have received and analyzed them, prepared its own countervaluations of thousands of securities, and hurriedly presented them at the hearing. That afternoon the judge can review voluminous filings, arrive at reasoned conclusions and findings, and write an explanatory opinion of a denial in a couple of hours, or give up and simply rule that with so much paperwork no action can possibly be arbitrary, or just let the clock run out at five o'clock instead of serving as a rubber stamp.[6]

What about postseizure judicial review, as some emergency circumstances can justify? The reviewing courts are limited to the same truncated and one-sided record and a dilemma as to any real relief. Though they can take more time, they are prohibited from issuing any stays, and liquidation is meanwhile mandated to be proceeding apace. And even if somehow a final ruling were in the company's favor, irreparable damage would already have occurred. Nor could the company simply sue the United States for monetary compensation for a due process violation[7]—it would likely claim sovereign immunity.[8]

---

6. The Supreme Court has recognized, but did not have to reach, the due process question of "whether the time is so short that it deprives litigants of a meaningful opportunity to be heard." *Miller v. French*, 530 U.S. 327, 350 (2000). In a separate opinion, Justice Souter suggested that providing insufficient time for a court to make a determination could raise "a serious question whether Congress has in practical terms assumed the judicial function." *Id.* at 352.

7. Note that any action would have to be against the government for its seizure, not against the FDIC for its decisions on claims against the company in receivership.

8. There is apparently no Tucker Act damage remedy for violations of Fifth Amendment due process: *Scheafnocker v. C.I.R.* 642 F.3d 426, 434 (3d Cir. 2011); *Smith v. U.S.*, 51 Fed. Cl. 36, 38 (2001). Perhaps a "takings" claim could be maintained, but it would face the assertion that Congress had excluded that remedy, by providing an exclusive avenue of appeal from a "final" decision. § 202(a)(1)(B). Nor would there be a likely remedy under the Federal Tort Claims Act. *See U.S. v.*

Note that none of these problems would arise if the company were simply put into judicial bankruptcy proceedings, as in fact was Lehman Brothers. And it is hard to find actual disasters occasioned by the Lehman process itself—as opposed to the shock to the markets that the government was not coming to the rescue, as it had with Bear Stearns.[9] There are desirable adjustments to the Bankruptcy Code that could somewhat reduce spillover effects in such cases. But if the Dodd-Frank procedure meets constitutional requirements, there is not much left of the Due Process Clause for financial companies.

Gaubert, 499 U.S. 319 (1991). That act contains an exception for "discretionary functions," even if the discretion is abused. 28 U.S.C. § 2680(a).

9. *See, e.g.,* Kimberly Summe, *Lessons Learned from the Lehman Bankruptcy*, in *Ending Government Bailouts* (Kenneth Scott, George Shultz, & John Taylor, eds., Hoover Institution Press, 2010).

POSTLOGUE

8

Regulatory Reform

A Practitioner's Perspective

Kevin M. Warsh

The events of the past several years make a compelling case for comprehensive, fundamental reform in the oversight of financial firms.

But I worry that the Dodd-Frank Act may not be equal to this critical task. As currently envisaged, Dodd-Frank seems premised on the notion that more regulators from more agencies with more funding, power, and discretion will stop financial firms from getting into trouble. That enhanced regulatory discipline alone—more "boots on the ground" and more exacting checklists to police financial firms—will ensure that financial firms remain safe and sound. If this theory has it right, next time will indeed be different.

My experience at the Federal Reserve informs my views on prudential oversight, leaving me with three key takeaways: First, most banking regulators are very knowledgeable, highly dedicated professionals with the utmost integrity. Second, the business of banking can thrive with clear rules of the road that prejudice no particular firm or function. And, third, the paradigm that leaves the overwhelming burden of prudential supervision on the judgments of regulators and supervisors alone is bound to disappoint.

Regulatory discipline has an important role to play, of course. But two other essential, complementary pillars of prudential supervision must be resurrected rather than relegated: capital standards and market discipline. As I discuss subsequently, neither clearer capital rules nor effective market discipline can be made operative when the largest U.S. firms are deemed "too big to fail." Of course, Dodd-Frank nominally purports to end the "too big to fail" doctrine, but in practice—now more than ever—it is viewed by market participants as *de facto* government policy. The window of opportunity to eradicate this problem is fleeting, so the time for more rigorous scrutiny of the new regulatory regime is at hand.

A more robust reform agenda—including but not limited to the introduction of Chapter 14 as an amendment to the Bankruptcy Code—should be targeted at ridding us of "too big to fail" firms. Clearer, tougher, and more assured treatment of stakeholders in large financial institutions—known and understood prior to the onset of distress—would go some distance toward mitigating the "too big to fail" problem at the core of our financial system.

If true reforms were implemented, the three independent pillars of prudential supervision—regulatory discipline, capital standards, and market discipline—could be revived to better serve their essential, complementary roles. This would go a long way toward re-energizing the U.S. banking system and providing the impetus the U.S. economy needs to flourish.

We cannot have a durable, competitive, dynamic banking system that facilitates economic growth if policy protects the franchises of oligopolies atop the financial sector. And our government—short of fiscal space—should not put itself in the position of directing policy through quasi-public banking utilities.

CAPITAL STANDARDS

The proposed capital regime suffers from some infirmities—each of which may ultimately undermine this important prudential pillar from being made durable and effective. As a result, I worry that recent capital rules are at some risk of being gamed, feigned, or deferred in the years ahead.

First, U.S. regulators, working with their international compatriots as part of the Basel Committee, established a joint accord (Basel III) for capital, ostensibly with full implementation set for 2019. Surely, a mutually agreed international framework is a noble and worthwhile objective. But the banking model of many foreign sovereigns is fundamentally different from that to which the United States should aspire. Some advanced foreign economies tend to be dominated by near-permanent oligopolistic banking systems, sanctioned and supported by their sovereigns. And most of those firms tend to be far larger relative to their home country's gross domestic product (GDP) than is the case in the United States. As a result, many of those with whom the United States negotiates implementation of capital standards may hold very different preferences and priorities. This makes a robust global accord problematic—especially at a time when many foreign banks are thought to be undercapitalized and their economies underperforming—and likely subject to continuous revision and reinterpretation.

Second, the current Basel capital-setting regime—like its predecessors—may lead to massively complex and opaque capital standards. This makes capital levels difficult for regulators to calibrate among regulated firms, infeasible for international bodies to assess across countries, and almost impossible for investors to understand and rely upon in evaluating individual firms. "Regulatory capital" is a less-reliable bulwark against economic weakness than actual shareholders' capital that can absorb actual losses. Consequently, I prefer a simpler, more straightforward, risk-sensitive, and more readily reviewable capital standard.

Third, capital levels post-Dodd-Frank are being tasked with a role well beyond their traditional remit of ensuring safety and soundness. Supervisors are being asked to assign extra capital cushions to systemically important financial institutions (SIFIs) so that larger, more interconnected institutions hold commensurately more capital to compensate for the greater risk to the financial system. These so-called SIFI buffers are an understandable attempt to level the playing field. But it is a very distant next-best to ridding the U.S. financial system of large, quasi-public utilities atop the sector. In practice, a couple of percentage points of incremental regulatory capital at inception are unlikely to persist as memories of the crisis fade. And by acknowledging that some select firms are systemically important, I worry that it will only memorialize "too big to fail" firms at the core of banking and reinforce the notion to creditors and counterparties that the government is unwilling to let them suffer losses.

Instead, the United States and other willing countries should begin from a first-best foundation with strong, simple, transparent capital standards appropriate for a dynamic, competitive banking system. This type of capital regime would be well positioned to attract customers and counterparties from around the world. As progress is achieved, I would expect an international coalition to join these efforts.

MARKET DISCIPLINE

In addition to improved regulatory discipline and clearer capital standards, the third and final pillar of prudential supervision—market discipline—must be revived. Market prices of financial firms should reveal much about their standing. Markets can help discipline the behavior of firms by repricing funding costs as perceived risks change. And stakeholders—that is, shareholders, creditors, and regulators alike—can use changes in market prices to evaluate the changing financial position of firms.

However, market discipline will only prove effective if stakeholders gain information to compare firms' exposures against one another in a timely and effective manner. The Federal Reserve's most recent stress tests—particularly the enhanced disclosure—are a step in the right direction. Still, disclosure practices by the largest financial firms remain lacking and the periodic reporting overseen by the Securities and Exchange Commission (SEC) tends to obfuscate more than inform. I favor a far more sweeping transparency initiative so that the financial statements and associated risks of large, complex firms can be monitored effectively by market participants.

But even if market participants possessed the information to better assess firms' standings, market discipline might still be unable to exert influence. Repeated government interventions during the financial crisis, whether advisable or not, revealed a set of policy preferences. Expectations hardened—in the United States and elsewhere—that governments will come to the rescue of large, failing firms. The result is a U.S. banking system that is now more concentrated, and the government's support of our largest banks is even more assured. These expectations must be unlearned by market participants. If not, market discipline will not be operative.

Bigness in financial services is not badness. But our largest financial firms must be able to persuade regulators that their failure would not endanger the financial markets and broader economy. Some of our largest banks are likely to pass this test, and would turn out to be more successful without implicit government support. Others, however, might not pass muster. Hence, the scale and scope of some firms would necessarily diminish. So be it.

Those "interconnected" firms that find themselves dependent on implicit government support do not serve our economy's interest. Their continued existence should not be countenanced. The risks associated with our largest firms must never again be underwritten by taxpayers. Those of us who were long worried about the systemic risks posed by Fannie Mae and Freddie Mac should be no less troubled if our largest banks are effectively backed by the U.S. government.

Eradicating the notion of "too big to fail" firms is the *sine qua non* to bring about real reform of financial services. Some progress has been made by the Federal Deposit Insurance Corporation (FDIC) in preparing protocols to resolve large firms. I am also particularly impressed by the work being done by the Financial Stability Board's Resolution Steering Group. But other regulatory initiatives strike me as going in a less-constructive direction. For example, by sanctioning a list of "too big to fail" firms—and treating them differently than the rest—policy makers are signaling to markets that the government is vested in their survival.

ORDERLY LIQUIDATION AUTHORITY

When the regulatory reform debate began, Congress appeared keen to ensure that there would be no more bailouts and no institutions would be "too big to fail," but even today the doctrine persists. Hence, the three pillars of prudential supervision are not being deployed most constructively to oversee financial firms.

Title II of Dodd-Frank establishes the option of an Orderly Liquidation Authority (OLA), ostensibly to resolve failing financial firms that are determined to pose a significant risk to financial stability. If the OLA is invoked by the Secretary of the Treasury, based on the recommendations of the Federal Reserve and the FDIC (or in some cases, the SEC or the new Federal Insurance Office), extraordinary powers are granted—including the ability to obtain bridge funding from the Treasury—to preserve franchise value and facilitate a transfer to a purchaser. Of note, Dodd-Frank also allows the FDIC to make payments to certain creditors.

In retrospect, could bank regulators and administration officials have employed the OLA to handle Bear Stearns or Lehman Brothers more effectively? This sort of authority might well have proven useful during the recent financial crisis. If we had gone into the crisis with the resolution authority outlined by the OLA, there may well have been better options to ensure an orderly disposition of failing firms. I suspect that the OLA would have been an attractive—but highly debated—alternative. Those favoring its use would have had a more compelling argument if it had long been the law of the land and understood by market participants to be an integral and preferred part of policy makers' tool kit. But if this form of liquidation were only a newly established authority in an unpracticed statute, some other policy makers might have considered it too risky to invoke. Still, if nothing else, the OLA could have strengthened the regulators' negotiating posture with certain financial firms.

Many supporters of Dodd-Frank argue that the OLA would have substantially mitigated the harm inflicted by the financial crisis. Even if they are correct about its effects in war-gaming the last crisis, this new grant of discretionary authority is unlikely to be up to the task going forward. There is no going home again. The status quo *ante* will no longer do.

Placing this arrow in the quiver of policy makers now is not sufficient to arm them for the challenges ahead. Granting new powers to resolve failing firms in the discretionary hands of regulators is unlikely to drive the market discipline required to avoid the recurrence of financial crises. The significant regulatory discretion built into Dodd-Frank is unlikely to dissuade investors from their learned view—however debatable it might be—that the government will stand behind its largest banks. Creditors will be protected, they will figure. And they might turn out to be correct.

We have to stop fighting the last war. As Governor Mark Carney, the head of the Financial Stability Board, reminds us, too often policies are put into place that would have mitigated the last crisis, but leave policy makers exceptionally vulnerable to the next one.

CHAPTER 14

There is no single panacea to deal with financial crises, but invoking a new Chapter 14 of the Bankruptcy Code would be a very useful step forward, particularly as part of a true reform package to strengthen the dynamism and resiliency of the banking system.

The Bankruptcy Code brings with it precedent, case law, and well-understood protocols to provide substantial clarity as to the rights and obligations of each class of stakeholders. It has a deep history of respect for the rule of law without favor or prejudice. In fact, reliable treatment under our Bankruptcy Code—and respect for the rule of law—distinguishes us from some foreign economies and attracts capital to our shores.

A new chapter of the Bankruptcy Code—applicable to all financial institutions—would bring much-needed credibility to the murky issues involving the government's support of large financial firms. A Chapter 14 amendment to the code would go some distance toward reminding creditors and counterparties that the government has fine, effective, and well-understood options to unwind a financial firm and, in the long run, to promote financial stability.

The benefits associated with Chapter 14 go well beyond establishing clarity about how failing financial firms would be unwound. It is about ridding markets of "too big to fail" expectations in the near term. It is about changing behavior in good times so that the bad times are less bad. Early assessments of financial firms—and vibrant competition among them—will better ensure that we do not find ourselves in another banking crisis. Hence, the tougher, clearer, less-discretionary measures, including invoking Chapter 14, would represent a substantial improvement in existing law.

So, what if Chapter 14 were available to policy makers alongside the OLA? To achieve meaningful benefits, Chapter 14 would have to be understood as the prevailing, dominant option. If investors believed that the OLA was more likely to be used by policy makers than the "tough love" of Chapter 14, its benefits would quickly dissipate.

Ultimately, my preference for Chapter 14 versus a newfangled liquidation authority is based, in part, on my strong bias that the existence of large, quasi-public utilities atop the financial sector is growth-defeating for the U.S. economy. Those who prefer the OLA put greater emphasis on wanting to preserve optionality and flexibility going into the next crisis.

I, however, am more willing to constrain discretion and return to a clearer, more rules-based oversight regime that relies more on real capital and true market forces. In so doing, the United States will have a stronger, more dynamic and competitive banking system to serve the interests of consumers, businesses, and the broader economy.

9

A Macroeconomic Perspective

"Dealing with Too Big to Fail"

ANDREW CROCKETT

The existence of financial institutions that are perceived as too big (or too important) to be allowed to fail can impose economic costs by enhancing the incentives for socially undesirable risk taking. If providers of funds to financial institutions regard themselves as protected by the prospect of government support, they will be willing to commit more resources and engage in less oversight than if they believe borrowers will be subject to normal commercial disciplines. As a result, some "too big to fail" institutions may be tempted to assume higher levels of risk than warranted by optimal resource allocation. To the extent that this is true, economic distortions are created while such institutions are active, and a potential charge on taxpayers arises when they run into difficulties. Prudently managed and successful enterprises, of whatever size, are penalized by comparison.

It should not be difficult, therefore, to agree on the principle that all institutions in a competitive market economy should face the threat of failure as a result of bad business judgment. Indeed, it will not be possible to say that a financial system is fully capable of meeting its function of guiding resources to their most efficient uses until the anomaly of "too big to fail" is dealt with. This is, in fact, a major goal of much financial reform legislation being enacted around the world.

To make the threat of failure credible, however, it must be possible for any troubled financial institution that cannot be recapitalized as a going concern to be sold, merged, or wound down without creating unacceptable costs or risks to the broader economy. This is not perceived to be the case at present. Despite legislative initiatives following the recent crisis, many observers believe that governments would nevertheless feel obliged to step in to protect key financial institutions during future periods of stress. They argue that the failure of a large and interconnected institution would be so disruptive to the financial system in general that, whatever governments might say now, they will feel obliged to intervene in the event of crisis to support such institutions.

A corollary of this argument is the view that the institutions concerned should either be broken up or carry such high levels of equity capital as to be effectively safe from failure. But such a policy prescription carries its own risks of resource misallocation by (1) diverting possibly excessive levels of capital into financial intermediation, (2) distorting competition between regulated and unregulated institutions, and (3) substituting administrative judgment for market processes in determining the most efficient structure of the financial industry. Developing techniques to make failure a tolerable option—such as the new Chapter 14 of the U.S. Bankruptcy Code, discussed in chapter 2—would not only restore market discipline and protect taxpayers but also avoid potentially costly measures that seek to eliminate the possibility of failure.

An important consideration that can lead to an institution being viewed as too important to fail is the degree of its interconnectedness with other parts of the financial system. The more that one institution's distress is perceived as creating problems for others, the greater the expectation it may have to be rescued by the authorities.

It is therefore of key importance to reduce the vulnerabilities created by interconnectedness as much as possible.

In a modern financial system, of course, institutions are connected by a variety of trading links and counterparty relationships. These links are essential for risk management and diversification, as well as for efficient credit allocation. There are, however, techniques for reducing gross exposures through netting and the use of central counterparties (CCPs). By utilizing a small number of CCPs, managed and regulated separately from the institutions that use their services, the overall exposures in the system may be reduced considerably. Much reform effort has therefore been devoted to channeling transactions toward regulated exchanges, central clearinghouses, and real-time settlement systems. Standardization of transaction instruments is helpful in this regard, though it should not prevent the creation of bespoke transactions where this is warranted.

Of course, the reduction of risk for trading institutions is achieved by concentrating exposures within clearing and settlement systems. It will also be important, therefore, to have robust oversight of CCPs and well-conceived recovery and resolution plans in case these institutions themselves encounter difficulties. It is probably also necessary to have a suitable safety net in place to ensure that key functions performed by infrastructure utilities are not interrupted. Admittedly, this may lead to moral hazard, but moral hazard is a less-pressing concern when the entity involved is a regulated utility rather than a purely profit-maximizing enterprise. Indeed, it may be worth considering whether a not-for-profit model might be more suitable for certain key infrastructures.

Even if the transactional infrastructure is strengthened in the way just suggested, financial institutions will still be vulnerable to periodic stress, and the authorities will need to respond when they are. The issue is complicated by the currently well-recognized fact that standard bankruptcy procedures are not well suited for financial institutions. A financial institution cannot function in bankruptcy in the same way as a commercial enterprise. It cannot obtain temporary protection from its creditors because access by creditors is its raison d'être. As a result, when bankruptcy occurs, it is liable to be much more disruptive to the institution's creditors and counterparties than is the case with a nonfinancial enterprise. Moreover, when the institution concerned is large, it may play such a pivotal role in an economy that the government may be reluctant to accept the consequences of its failure. Such potential systemic consequences have motivated past rescues of troubled financial institutions.

These considerations suggest that, to make the ending of "too big to fail" truly credible, a specialized resolution regime for large financial institutions needs to be developed. Such an approach (as discussed in chapter 2) could involve a special chapter of the U.S. Bankruptcy Code that takes account of the specific characteristics of large financial institutions. Such a resolution regime would need to ensure that an institution encountering difficulties could continue to serve socially essential functions and would not be liquidated in a manner that disrupted financial intermediation more generally or destroyed value unnecessarily. Moreover, to avoid moral hazard, it would require that owners and creditors of the institution bore losses that were predictable and in accordance with their position within the capital structure of the enterprise. It would need to protect taxpayers from direct losses due to the provision of solvency support, as well as, to the extent possible, indirect losses due to the wider economic effects of the enterprise's failure. Finally, for globally active institutions, it would need to ensure there was a mechanism that defined fairly the relative roles of the authorities in each of the jurisdictions in which the institution was active.

It is important to note that, for a financial institution, "failure" does not inevitably mean bankruptcy and immediate liquidation. It can cover a number of different responses to a situation in which the enterprise is unable to continue operating in its preexisting form. The possibility of failure arises whenever a financial institution faces difficulties in attracting funding to meet its commitments. There are a variety of possible responses to such a situation—which means there would need to be a variety of tools to secure a socially optimal result in particular circumstances. These tools fall loosely into two categories: (1) "recovery" of the troubled institution through sale as a going concern or recapitalization, and (2) "resolution" through breaking it up and liquidating some or all of its assets.

Normally, it would be preferable to first attempt to sell a troubled institution to a stronger competitor, which may be possible if it has a strong franchise value, and provided there are no negative consequences from a competition perspective. Naturally, the search for an acquirer would have to start well in advance of the prospect of imminent failure, and may be facilitated by actions from the firm's supervisor. It is important, however, for any official assistance to avoid financial commitments that, in effect, bail out creditors of the failing firm. If no purchaser is available or suitable, another approach is to write down the value of existing unsecured debt (or convert part or all of it to equity) in a sufficient amount to restore the viability of the enterprise. This would have to be done in such a way that no creditor would be disadvantaged by comparison with their position in liquidation. Again, to avoid moral hazard, taxpayer funds should not be put at risk, though temporary liquidity, suitably collateralized support need not be ruled out.

Only if sale or recovery is impossible would it become necessary to "resolve" a failing institution. But resolution is unlikely to be most efficiently accomplished by immediate liquidation. There will almost certainly be activities that can be spun off and made profitable; and there may be other activities that are deemed essential from a social point of view (e.g., utility functions, such as clearing and settlement). Even those activities that are deemed nonviable in the longer term may well involve avoidable social costs if terminated abruptly.

Part of any resolution regime should therefore be to develop techniques that enable certain functions of a failing financial institution to continue to be performed, while running down over time those activities or parts of the balance sheet that have become unviable. At the same time, to avoid moral hazard, it is essential that equity and debt holders bear their appropriate share of the losses involved. The first loss should always fall on equity owners, with further losses being borne by subordinated debt holders, unsecured creditors, and so on up the capital structure.

One means of resolving a troubled financial institution while maintaining incentives and preserving as much value as possible— which has been successfully applied in a number of countries—is to separate the balance sheet into a "good bank" and a "bad bank." The good bank would retain the assets that continue to perform in accordance with their contractual terms, along with their sources of funding (which, in the case of a bank, would include insured deposits). Such an institution would be potentially profitable and, perhaps after a period of publicly provided liquidity support, could be returned to full private ownership relatively quickly. The bad bank would contain most of the impaired assets, together with, on the liability side of its balance sheet, the subordinated and unguaranteed sources of funding. These assets would be run down over time (in order to maximize recovery values) and the creditors repaid whatever share of their investment was realizable from asset sales.

The creation of a good bank and its eventual return to full private ownership helps answer the concern that the failure of an institution may have an adverse effect on competition within the industry. In those countries where banking systems are already concentrated, there is understandable worry that the disappearance of a major institution would add to oligopoly risks. To the extent that this is a valid concern, other techniques are available to combat it. The competition authorities can prevent the sale of the troubled institution to a dominant competitor and provide instead for independence under new ownership.

In order to achieve the objectives of orderly resolution of a large financial institution facing distress, a clear legislative framework would need to be put in place. Ideally, such a framework would promote certainty by limiting the amount of discretion the authorities could apply in implementing the framework (although it is probably unrealistic to eliminate discretion entirely). A key requirement, as I have already emphasized, would be to enforce losses in accordance with the capital structure of the institution in difficulties.

Such a framework would also need to distinguish between those claims on the institution that would be subject to a "stay" in bankruptcy and those that could be immediately exercised. This is not a simple judgment, as other chapters in this volume make clear. The recent crisis revealed the dangers of exempting illiquid securities from stays. The liquidity of the claims secured by such instruments as collateralized debt obligations depends crucially on the marketability of the underlying instrument. When this comes into question, say because of uncertainty about valuations, creditors demand greater collateral margin (haircuts). However, posting additional collateral immediately squeezes the liquidity of the borrower, prompting concerns about its funding strategy. As the process unfolds, a vicious spiral sets in—which, in the recent crisis, led to a freezing up of the repo market and was a major factor in the failure or near failure of key market players. It thus seems desirable that exemption from stays should be limited to those securities that, with high confidence, will maintain their credit standing and marketability.

Nonexempt transactions would be subject to the normal stay in bankruptcy, going with the bad bank to be liquidated over time with the objective of maximizing value. The bad bank might need liquidity support to finance its portfolio over the period in which its assets were being liquidated. This amount would be small if creditors were only paid out of the proceeds of sales as they occurred, but it could be larger if creditors were allowed early access to funds, based on an estimate of recovery values. This might be desirable to alleviate stress among the creditors. The interest of taxpayers could be protected by employing conservative values for assets, combined perhaps with "clawback" provisions in case recovery values proved to be overestimated. A further protection could be provided by requiring any residual loss to become a charge on the industry. However, this does not fully address the problem of moral hazard, as prudent "survivors" in effect become providers of funds to the less-prudent "victims."

An important issue arises concerning the treatment of the management of a distressed financial institution. Some of the legislation enacted following the recent crisis seems based on a desire to ensure that management is "punished" for its failures. Thus, it is proposed that in future failures, management should be relieved of its position immediately. Although this motivation is understandable, it would be more appropriate, and help to maximize recovery values, to adopt a pragmatic approach. Given that the franchise value of a financial institution is significantly dependent on the human capital of its senior management, there is a case for allowing such capital to be retained as long as necessary to realize the greatest value from ongoing operations.

A final issue arises regarding institutions with international operations. Different legislative philosophies across different jurisdictions complicate the task of ensuring equal treatment in resolution for creditors of large global financial institutions. Realistically, it is highly unlikely that full legislative harmonization will be achieved any time soon. Some observers consider that this points to ring fencing subsidiaries so that each could be resolved within a single national jurisdiction. While this would help, it would not be a full solution and, in any case, it would work against some of the economies that come with cross-border operation.

A better solution would be to make use of the fact that all major jurisdictions are in the process of developing special resolution regimes for large and complex financial institutions, and attempting to make these regimes mutually consistent and supportive. This would include, *inter alia*, provisions for information sharing (both during crises and in "peacetime"), protocols governing common treatment of creditors in different jurisdictions, preexisting understandings (perhaps developed through "living wills") about how a distressed institution would be resolved, and so on.

None of this will be easy. But the Financial Stability Board has provided a set of "Key Attributes" of recovery and resolution regimes that give grounds to hope that, with effort and goodwill, the issue of "too big to fail" can finally be put to rest. Full acceptance that it has ended will probably have to await a successful resolution of a failing institution without taxpayer costs or systemic fallout. But in the meantime, participants in financial markets should be encouraged to act as though the creditors of a stressed institution will no longer be bailed out by the authorities.

About the Authors

Andrew Crockett is special adviser to the chairman at JPMorgan Chase. Crockett previously served as general manager of the Bank for International Settlements (1993–2003) and as first chairman of the Financial Stability Forum (now the Financial Stability Board) (1999–2003). Earlier in his career, Crockett held positions at the Bank of England and the International Monetary Fund. His research interest is financial regulation. He was educated at Cambridge and Yale Universities and was knighted in 2003. He is a member of the Hoover Institution's Working Group on Economic Policy.

Darrell Duffie is the Dean Witter Distinguished Professor in Finance at the Graduate School of Business, Stanford University. Duffie is a member of the Financial Advisory Roundtable of the Federal Reserve Bank of New York and a member of the Board of Directors of Moody's Corporation. He serves on the boards of scholarly journals in finance, economics, and mathematics, and was elected president of the American Finance Association for 2009. He is a fellow and member of the Council of the Econometric Society, a fellow of the American Academy of Arts and Sciences, and a research associate of the National Bureau of Economic Research. Duffie is a coauthor of *The Squam Lake Report: Fixing the Financial System* (Princeton University Press, 2010). His other recent books include *How Big Banks Fail* (Princeton University Press, 2010), *Measuring Corporate Default Risk* (Oxford University Press, 2011), and *Dark Markets* (Princeton University Press, 2012). He received his PhD from Stanford in 1984.

Thomas H. Jackson, university professor at the University of Rochester, served as president of the university from 1994 to 2005. Before he became Rochester's ninth president, Jackson was vice president and provost of the University of Virginia, which he first joined in 1988 as dean of Virginia's School of Law. He had been professor of law at Harvard from 1986 to 1988 and served on the Stanford University faculty from 1977 to 1986. A 1972 graduate of Williams College, Jackson earned his law degree from Yale in 1975. He first clerked for U.S. District Court judge Marvin E. Frankel in New York in 1975–76, and then for Supreme Court Justice (later Chief Justice) William H. Rehnquist in 1976–77. The author of bankruptcy and commercial law texts used in law schools across the country, he served as Special Master for the U.S. Supreme Court in a dispute involving every state in the country over the disposition of unclaimed dividends held by brokerage houses.

William F. Kroener III is counsel at Sullivan & Cromwell LLP. He served as general counsel of the Federal Deposit Insurance Corporation from 1995 to 2006. His law practice focuses on the supervision and regulation of banks and other regulated financial institutions and their advisers. Kroener currently serves as cochair of the American Bar Association Presidential Task Force on Financial Markets Regulatory Reform, chair of the Banking Law Committee of the American Bar Association Business Law Section, an advisory member of the Financial Institutions Committee of the Business Law Section of the State Bar of California, and a member of the Regulatory Appeals Committee of the Dubai Financial Services Authority. He speaks and writes regularly on financial regulatory topics and has taught as an adjunct professor at Stanford, George Washington, and American University law schools. Kroener is a graduate of Yale and Stanford law and business schools.

Kenneth E. Scott, the Parsons Professor Emeritus of Law and Business at Stanford Law School and a Hoover Institution senior research fellow, is a leading scholar in the fields of corporate finance reform and corporate governance who has written extensively on federal banking regulation. His current research concentrates on legislative and policy developments related to the current financial crisis, comparative corporate governance, and financial regulation. Scott is the editor (with George Shultz and John Taylor) of the recent book *Ending Government Bailouts* (2010). He has extensive consulting experience, including work for the World Bank, the Federal Deposit Insurance Corporation, the Resolution Trust Corporation, and, most recently, the National Association of Securities Dealers (now FINRA). He is also a member of the Shadow Financial Regulatory Committee, the Financial Economists Roundtable, and the State Bar of California's Financial Institutions Committee. Before joining the Stanford Law School faculty in 1968, Scott served as general counsel to the Federal Home Loan Bank Board and as chief deputy savings and loan commissioner of California and worked in private practice in New York with Sullivan & Cromwell.

David Skeel is the S. Samuel Arsht Professor of Corporate Law at the University of Pennsylvania Law School. He is the author of *The New Financial Deal: Understanding the Dodd-Frank Act and Its (Unintended) Consequences* (Wiley, 2011), *Icarus in the Boardroom: The Fundamental Flaws in Corporate America and Where They Came From* (Oxford University Press, 2005), *Debt's Dominion: A History of Bankruptcy Law in America* (Princeton University Press, 2001), and numerous articles on bankruptcy, corporate law, Christianity and law, and other topics. Skeel has also written commentaries for the *New York Times, Wall Street Journal, Books & Culture, Weekly Standard,* and other publications.

Kimberly Anne Summe is the chief operating officer and general counsel of Partner Fund Management, a San Francisco–based investment adviser. She is also a lecturer in law at the Stanford Law School. Summe was previously a managing director in prime brokerage at Lehman Brothers, prior to which she served as general counsel of the

International Swaps and Derivatives Association. In the latter capacity, Summe was responsible for developing industry-standard contracts for the over-the-counter derivatives industry, as well as addressing regulatory issues in dozens of jurisdictions. She was a banking associate at Pillsbury Winthrop and Sullivan & Cromwell, and has published more than a dozen articles on various banking and securities law topics. Summe's interest in the capital markets has led her to establish a non-profit organization, Paladin Connect, which offers the pro bono services of leading global law firms to microfinance institutions. Summe received her law degrees from the University of Chicago and Cambridge University and a postgraduate degree from the London School of Economics.

John B. Taylor is the George P. Shultz Senior Fellow in Economics at the Hoover Institution and the Mary and Robert Raymond Professor of Economics at Stanford University. He is an award-winning teacher and researcher, specializing in macroeconomics, international economics, and monetary policy. Among other roles in public service, he served as a senior economist (1976–77) and as a member (1989–91) of the President's Council of Economic Advisers and as undersecretary of the Treasury for international affairs (2001–2005). Taylor's book *Getting Off Track: How Government Actions and Interventions Caused, Prolonged, and Worsened the Financial Crisis* was one of the first on the financial crisis; he has since followed up with two books on preventing future crises, coediting *The Road Ahead for the Fed* and *Ending Government Bailouts as We Know Them,* in which leading experts examine and debate proposals for financial reform and exit strategies. Before joining the Stanford faculty in 1984, Taylor held positions as a professor of economics at Princeton University and Columbia University. He received a BA in economics summa cum laude from Princeton and a PhD in economics from Stanford University in 1973.

Kevin M. Warsh is a distinguished visiting fellow at the Hoover Institution and a lecturer at the Stanford Graduate School of Business. He served as a member of the Board of Governors of the Federal Reserve System from 2006 to 2011. He focused on financial markets and the conduct of monetary policy. Warsh served as the Federal Reserve's representative to the Group of Twenty (G-20) and the board's emissary to the emerging and advanced economies in Asia. As the administrative governor, he managed and oversaw the board's operations, personnel, and financial performance. Before his appointment to the board (2002–2006), Warsh was the special assistant to the president for economic policy and executive secretary of the White House National Economic Council. Previously, he was a member of the Mergers and Acquisitions Department at Morgan Stanley & Co. in New York, serving as vice president and executive director. Warsh received his AB from Stanford University and his JD from Harvard Law School.

About the Hoover Institution's

WORKING GROUP ON ECONOMIC POLICY

THE WORKING GROUP ON ECONOMIC POLICY conducts research on current financial conditions as well as prevailing economic policies and issues, including domestic and global monetary, fiscal, and regulatory policies. Ideas that examine market and government dimensions of solutions are promoted, with the goal of increasing the extent and breadth of national and global prosperity.

For 25 years starting in the early 1980s, the U.S. economy experienced an unprecedented economic boom. Economic expansions were stronger and longer than in the past. Recessions were shorter, shallower, and less frequent. Gross domestic product (GDP) doubled and household net worth increased by 250 percent in real terms. Forty-seven million jobs were created.

This quarter-century boom strengthened as its length increased. Productivity growth surged by one full percentage point per year in the United States, creating an additional $9 trillion of goods and services that would never have existed. And the long boom went global, with emerging-market countries from Asia to Latin America to Africa experiencing the enormous improvements in both economic growth and economic stability.

Economic policies that place greater reliance on the principles of free markets, price stability, and flexibility have been the key to these successes. Recently, however, several powerful new economic forces have begun to change the economic landscape, and these principles are being challenged with far-reaching implications for U.S. economic policy, both domestic and international. A financial crisis flared up in 2007 and turned into a severe panic in 2008, leading to the Great Recession. How we interpret and react to these forces—and in particular whether proven policy principles prevail going forward—will determine whether strong economic growth and stability returns and again continues to spread and improve more people's lives or whether the economy stalls and stagnates.

Our Working Group organizes seminars and conferences, prepares policy papers and other publications, and serves as a resource for policy makers and interested members of the public.

THE RESOLUTION PROJECT

When in 2009 Congress began considering financial reforms proposed by the U.S. Treasury, a "resolution project" group was established, under the auspices of the Working Group on Economic Policy at the Hoover Institution at Stanford, to focus on alternative ways to deal with failing financial institutions. The group's members are Andrew Crockett, Darrell Duffie, Richard Herring, Thomas Jackson, William F. Kroener III, Kenneth E. Scott, George P. Shultz, David Skeel, Kimberly Anne Summe, and John B. Taylor.

The group held a number of meetings in the fall of 2009, which led to several papers and a conference in December 2009, the results of which were published in 2010 as *Ending Government Bailouts As We Know Them*, edited by Kenneth Scott, George Shultz, and John Taylor. The group continues to meet and work further on members' analyses and proposals; relevant papers will be posted at the Resolution Project website [http://www.hoover.org/taskforces/economic-policy/resolution-project/publications]. A proposal for modified bankruptcy procedures to better handle the failure of large, nonbank financial institutions, written by Tom Jackson, was the result of considerable discussions within the group.

Index